AF395502

REBIRTH AND RENEWAL

A JOURNEY IN SELF DISCOVERY

H. P. SINGH RISHI

BookLeaf Publishing

India | USA | UK

Rebirth and Renewal: A Journey in Self Discovery
© 2025
H. P. Singh Rishi

Presentation by *BookLeaf Publishing*

Web: www.bookleafpub.com
E-mail: info@bookleafpub.com

ISBN: 9789369542420

First edition 2025

*To the extraordinary women who have shaped my life
with their love strength and wisdom*

*Mandish Kaur – my mother
Ravinder Kaur – my wife
Dr Manasi Pritam and Major Shikha Chahal – my daughters
Veera Singh – my granddaughter*

*This book is a tribute to all of you, for you are the heartbeat
of my journey, the soul of my renewal and the reason
I strive to be better every day*

To Princess Ginger – my inspiration, my quiet muse, and the soul who taught me the true meaning of love

Reviews

The book celebrates boundless creativity of a remarkable soul who has enriched many lives.

    –Mona Singh. Partner MoMagic Foundations. NGO.

Rishis stories about Japan and its people are a fitting tribute to the country.

    –Y. Ota. Ex ITOCHU Corporation Japan.

A resilient courageous writer. Rishis stories are a lasting understanding of people of
different countries.

    –Vikas Gupta. Business Head of Habras International Ltd Dubai.

Gripping, invigorating, refreshing, motivating and stimulating. A must read for all
youngsters and young at heart

    –Prof Avinash Singh. Former Special Correspondent. Hindustan Times.

A wonderful book rooted in India and travel around the world.

    –Harpreet Singh Tv host. Surrey Canada.

Rishi is a maverick, a magician par excellence. A literary giant he communicates with
a sonorous voice rich in content.

–Lt. Col. Nageshwant Roy Vaid (Retd) Marketing strategist.

Real life practical experience. Rishi is a natural writer who writes from the heart. He takes you on a journey spanning the globe and shares his gripping experiences.

–Ron Wadhawan. Portfolio Manager.

What a beautiful portrait of live events.

–Dr Ashish Saberwal.

Rishis astute understanding of characters is amazing and so is his comprehension

–Ram Singh. Businessman.

Heart of 20 years and experience of 70. A movie can be made of some of the stories

–Rajiv Sethi. Chairman Kalinga Cables and Hotels.

Rishi has the art of coming out with a story so well that a reader could say, "Yeh dil maange more".

–P.P. Wangchuk. Ex Hindustan Times.

HPS - High profile Singh as I know him and as the Japanese knew him. Nothing was impossible for him.

–Debashish Chatterjee

The fabulous author who knows the pulse of the reader.

–Shamsher Singh. Nature poet.

A courageous brilliant determined writer who understands the psyche of Japan.

–Deepti Handa. UNDP.

Rishi juxtaposes life with laughter

–Seema Sethi. Housemaker.

Serendipity personified

–Manpreet Sharma. Consultant.

Rishi understands the Japanese business ethics and portrays them brilliantly

–Ashwini Menon. Ex ITOCHU Dubai.

The stories reflect that Rishi has a deep understanding of the challenges of life.

–Gurleen Kaur. British Airways.

Rishi portrays the hard and exciting life with a lot of struggle and suffering.

–Satpal Kaily. Pharma business. Birmingham UK.

Real and moving stories from which you can gain a lot.

–Dr Vijai Vazirani. Prof of mathematics in USA.

Contents

PART XII

PART I

Silent Voice of Parents

I owe a debt of gratitude to my parents, who are no more, and I wish to place on record that the word gratitude or debt is a misnomer. No one, and I dare say no one, can repay the debt of gratitude to someone who has given you life, sustenance, knowledge-based upbringing, and courage to face the world. Words fail me as parents are the supreme manifestations of the Gods we never see but who live in us.

Parents are the Rocks of Gibraltar who help us to tide the storms of life, guide us during turbulent times, and pray for us when we are in trouble. They have no hidden agenda and are like the anchors of ships that dock at the harbour. They wait for us at home silently when we go to work and can tell from our faces whether we had a good day or not.

My parents were indulgent and spoiled me. They wanted me to become a teacher as they were both in the same profession. They told me I would remain young, and as I was fond of reading and writing, it suited my temperament. I did not listen to them. I paid a heavy price by spending three decades in the corporate world despite my heart not being in it. I aged much before my time, developed terrible eating habits, became obese, and now take about fifteen tablets daily. I lost much more than I gained in the process.

Fortunately, my parents taught me the values of integrity, generosity, respecting the have-nots, honesty, humility, adaptability, discipline, spirit, a winning mindset, and resilience. They were more on a friendly basis with me. They were my biggest inspiration engines and cheerleaders in whatever I did. They told me my forte was writing; I should focus on that as it would act as a catharsis. Thanks to them, I got into *ishq* mode with writing, which gave me much happiness.

I recall an incident from when I was once travelling.

'My son is 18 years old and is not leaving me.' I was stunned to hear this comment from a US national travelling with me on a flight.

'You should be happy, Sir, that your child is staying with you.'

'If he stays with me for long, he will never grow up. He will learn from the hard knocks of life and be a stronger man to confront life,' he answered.

'But I can never think of staying away from my parents.' It was the American's turn to be amazed now.

'Don't tell me your parents are staying with you?'

'I stay with them, Sir, and I am delighted.' The poor American, Tim, was dazed. He made several expressions with his face and looked at me with wonder in his eyes as if I was from a different planet.

'What is there for you in this arrangement?'

'Plenty, and most importantly, they are my parents, and I owe a lot to them. Our family is united, and I firmly believe that families that stay together are bonded and better than nuclear families.'

'What about your independence?'

'It is not blocked at all.'

'In what way?' asked Tim, with a puzzled look on his face.

'We have more time to pursue our chosen activities as we know that our house is in safe hands. I can excel more in my profession and pursue my passions because I do not have to look after the running of the house. My wife, a school teacher, can perform better in her job as she does not have to carry out the mundane, thankless jobs that are time-consuming but have to be done. Our kids can pursue their dreams of excellence in sports thanks to the support they get from their grandparents.'

'And may I ask how?'

'It is my father's responsibility to take my kids to the swimming pool about thirteen km from our house, at five am every day. He has done it six days a week for over five years. He has been making my kids eat a healthy breakfast after their strenuous training session prepared by my mother and wife together. He drops them at school after that and then returns home. One of us would surely have had to sacrifice their job to do that.'

'But don't you have fights?' Tim asked.

'Yes, plenty of them. We argue over small issues like which channel to run on the TV, issues of live-in relationships, age of marriage, choice of partners, but three generations agree to disagree on their viewpoints and move on.'

'I would like to visit your wonderful family one day,' he said.

'Sure, you are welcome,' I responded warmly.

October 20, 2019, was my 34th wedding anniversary and became the saddest day of my life as I lost my beloved mother on that fateful day. My father followed her barely three months later. We miss them a lot, but the greatest irony of life is that we manage to live on even without those we thought we could never do without. They come in my dreams and ask me if I am well. I will surely meet them in heaven one day when I go up there.

Dynamic Moms and Their Dilemma!

'Mother is a fact, father is a belief'
—Maxim Gorky.

'E maavan dhandian chaavan ne, behna nu kaya bhran ne,
Maa varga ghansavan boota mainu nazar na aaye, jiston le
ke chaan udhari Rab ne surg banaye.'

'Mothers are like cool shades, said the brothers to their
sisters,
I have not seen a more unique seed than a mother.
When Gods made heaven, they borrowed the shade for
it from mothers.'

I have noticed that, more often than not, mothers love
their sons more than daughters, and fathers love their
daughters more. Why? Mothers feel that the sons will
look after them in old age, and the fathers feel that the
daughter will leave the house after marriage and hence
deserves all the affection. It is a catch-22 situation.

A mother's job is selfless service at home whether
she is working or not. If she is 'just a housewife,' the
challenge is much more. She does a full-time job sans

much appreciation. She has to face the barbs sometimes. *'Aap karti hi kya ho? Office mein hazaaron kaam hote hain. Mein bahut thak jaata hun.'* What about the poor wife? She has to prepare food for the hubby and the kids in the morning, buy vegetables and fruit for the rest of the day, procure groceries, and clean the house. It leaves her hardly any time to rest.

A working woman has to balance the house and office like a trapeze artist. Adjusting with the mother-in-law, in case you are staying in a joint family, is a task as tricky as climbing Mt. Everest with your hands tied behind your back. The task is tougher if the husband is a *'paplu beta,'* i.e., mama's boy. She has to play the role of a commando then and take the right decisions instantly. One false move can have grave consequences.

While taking a walk in the park, I always put myself in the minds of people ahead of me or passing by. I am more interested in women in the *saaf dil* innocuous way. I accosted a young minus fifty woman with a spring in her step and asked her about her family. Suman lost her husband about four years ago and has one son, Lakshay, working for the Airport Authority of India. He has been admitted to the prestigious IIT Delhi for MS in Computer Science but desires to get into the flavour of the season, Artificial Intelligence.

Just like Ruskin Bond, I am computer illiterate. However, I have a keen desire to learn more and more. I requested Suman to fix a meeting with Lakshay, and the young boy was kind enough to come to our place. He was different; intelligent, handsome, quick-witted, always smiling, confident and focused. My first question to him was, 'Do you have a girlfriend, *beta?*' His response shocked me.

'I am 27. I want one, but I have deliberately decided to keep this time-consuming practice on hold. I will focus on more important things.' I was genuinely impressed.

However, I am worried about his mother. The young boy will live up to his name, but I can foresee him flying off to the USA to get a PhD and then getting a fab job there with plenty of money. What happens to Suman? She will be alone as he is the only child she has. I have seen it happening with my school and college friends who went to distant lands to chase their dreams and came to meet their parents once in a while or after they were gone to attend the last rites.

My prayers are there for the happiness of Suman and Lakshay. God has been unkind to Suman. She deserves loads of unlimited happiness.

What Does Your Father Mean to You?

*'Bete ko log kehte hain ke voh aankhon ka noor hai,
Hai zindagi ka lutf aur dil ka suroor hai.'*

The above lines hold more true for daughters than for sons.

My daughter, my biggest strength and weakness in life, wished me Happy Father's Day in the morning. She presented me with a pen from Roland Garros Paris, where she had gone for the French Open Tennis Tournament 2023, with a card stating more power to your pen. It was happiness personified. I requested her to put on my socks and shoes as I am very fat and have a bad muscle spasm making it impossible for me to bend. She willingly complied but with a rider. 'Papa, you are getting old.' I smiled weakly. My son, who is a *fauji* and posted in Mizoram also called. 'I am glad you are motivated at this age and also motivating others around you, Papa.' He made my day.

The vivid memory I have of my father is that he came to my school for a parent-teacher meeting when I was in sixth grade. While other parents were keen on knowing their kids' progress in their studies, my father was different. When my class teacher said, 'Rishi is a very quiet, obedient boy and does his homework on time,' my father's quick response shocked her and the parents around. 'This is a disqualification. I would have been delighted had you said that Rishi *bahut shararti hai.*' That was my father.

He was a true *karm yogi* who inspired me, motivated me, did not point out my stutter, and taught me how to ride a scooter and drive a car. When I banged the car on my first drive alone, he did not castigate me. He helped me overcome my speech impediment and pushed me to write by procuring many non-course books for me.

After retirement, he kept himself busy by walking every day with a stick and interacting with everyone around and being kind to the have-nots. I do the same. When my kids were hardly seven, he told me that he wanted them to become members of the winning teams of St. Stephen's College Delhi. Like an NDA instructor, he would wake them up at 4:30 am, take them to the swimming pool, give them breakfast, and drop them at school. Both became champs and captained their school and college teams to victory.

He would take two large pegs of Old Monk rum every day and sing songs of Heer Ranjha and Sassi Pannu. Unlike most fathers, he would encourage me to drink. 'What will you tell God? That I didn't drink and didn't enjoy life.' He drank till the age of 97 and was mentally and physically fit. He could not bear my mother's demise and left us barely three months after she passed away.

We celebrated his 100th anniversary on 1st April 2023 with a scintillating performance by Mantoo Veerji (Madan Gopal Singh) and his world-famous Chaar Yaar group. This was the best tribute to a man who did not deny age but defied it. Celebrate your parents' achievements while they are alive. Tell them that you love them. There is no point in praising them when they are no more.

I would be happy to know what you learnt from your father, what he meant to you, and how you are filling the void without him.

Parents and In-laws

Life and your parents are the biggest teachers, and your children are the biggest judges, *kyon ki,*
'Apne chehre ke daag kisko nazar aate hain,
Waqt har shaks ko asli chehra dikha deta hai.'

When you are young, you feel that you can conquer the world. At my age, the world conquers you. Everything is at your feet in your youth. Everyone around is at your beck and call. We take our parents for granted then and treat them as free servants whose only duty is to look after our needs.

During my walk in the morning, I see mothers feeding their kids food made with great love and care while waiting for school buses. The kids are reluctant to eat. I see mothers running after school buses with the heavy school bags of their children to stop them so they can go to the office after that. Sometimes their slippers are left behind. To hell with them. I witness fathers speeding up their cars after the school buses like Michael Schumacher. Will the kids remember all these sacrifices? I have my doubts.

As a rule, when you are in school or college, you berate your parents for being strict. 'Other parents are soooo good. They let their kids have night outs, buy them expensive cell phones, branded clothes, let them party, and procure bikes and cars for them. And you! *Humko humise kehte rehte ho ki paro aur paro and kuch ban jaao.* We are so unlucky.' The poor parents remain silent while getting the salvos from their kids.

And then you get married. *Sara sach saamne aa jata hai* when you start doing a comparison analysis. You have to be prim and proper while talking to your in-laws. You have to think five times before opening your mouth. You dare not confront your in-laws for fear of a battle royal with your spouse when you get home. You realise too late that your parents were very liberal, very accommodating. They listened to your bullshit and tried to accommodate your whims and fancies. Can you expect this treatment from your in-laws? No way!

I was allergic to head baths as my dense, long hair made it a complicated and difficult exercise. Until the age of 55, it was my mother's responsibility to give me a head bath. I would yell and shout like a little boy. *'Hai mar gaya.'*

My kids used to laugh at me. 'Papa, you are too dependent. You are a mamma's boy.' I was proud and happy to be one. For the last ten years, my wife has been religiously following the good practices of my mother every week. Would my mother-in-law have done the honours? Very doubtful. I wouldn't even have requested her.

I used to borrow my father's car in college; his office was right behind my college in Delhi Varsity. I would roam around with friends till late at night, and he would return home in an auto-rickshaw. He was a big sport. I could have never dared to borrow the car from my father-in-law though only God knows whether he would have given it. It is deja vu with my daughter. She has been using the family car as a birthright since college, whereas I have been happy travelling by Delhi Metro, e-rickshaws, and cabs if there is no connectivity.

Did my parents or I do right or wrong? There is nothing good or bad. It is only thinking that makes it so. Are you indulgent with your kids too? I am quite curious to know. *Kya yeh ghar ghar ki kahani hai Bharat main!*

PART II

A Salute to Indian Wives

Life is unpredictable and changes gears rapidly, just like Indian wives. They make you laugh and cry at the same time. They take you to the skies at one time and drop you to the bottomless pits of the earth at others. *Yahi Hindustani biwian hain!*

Marriage is a gamble. You will be very happy if it clicks. Otherwise, you become a philosopher like Socrates. They can give you *shanti* or make you suffer in the *safar* of life. They can become enduring happiness assets and force multipliers or heartaches who can make life extremely difficult. They are amazing and awesome at one time and can be a pain in the neck when the going gets tough.

They clear your head when it is in a muddle. They act as a soothing balm when your life is in tumultuous turmoil. They accept you with your deficiencies, spoil you, and make you move from areas of weakness to areas of strength.

The initial years of marriage can be pretty challenging, but the remaining roller coaster ride can become bliss if you play your cards correctly. It is an arduous journey that can become a joy if you accept your partners as they are. Powerful chemical attraction can be manufactured. You only have to make a sincere effort. The missing ingredients will melt with time, and you will become a fab couple.

It's extremely tough to be an Indian wife and equally challenging to be her lesser half. *Par dosto khushi paane ke liye jhukna parta hai.* Reinvent yourself from time to time. Radiate your life and make it shine by keeping your wife happy. Lift her spirits and adopt a win-win modus operandi. Attain Nirvana.

My father often reminded me, *'Rab da shukar kar Ravi ne tere nal vyah kar laya hega nahin tan tu chara hee mar jana si.'* He was absolutely right. A beautiful, intelligent spunky girl less than half my age with the sharp eyes of a film director, Mona Singh, used my father's words to make a 30-second documentary on us which got 25,000 views. And loads of happiness added. Thank you, Mona *beta.*

*'Haathon ki lakeeron se zindagi nahin banti
Azam hamara bhi hissa hai apni zindagi banane ka.'*

Dear hubbies, you have to make an effort to join the elite club of loving husbands I am in. Just Do It! Good L

Is Marriage a Setback?

It is a divine pact that culminates around a sacred fire, the priest or the Granth Sahib. In reel life, as a rule, marriage ends after the dancing part. But in real life, life starts after that. The mind-blowing rocking period turns into a mind-racking one when unpaid bills pile up and rent has to be paid if you don't own a house. And, if you are staying with parents sans pensions, it is another challenge. The loud rock music turns into a sombre mode, and the bickering begins.

The lovingly yours become grudgingly yours. Each partner starts stamping his or her authority on the relationship. It should not be so. The two partners are like the two wings of an aeroplane. They need to keep in tandem and strive to overcome the storms. If they rock the relationship like a boat does in a stormy sea, it spells doom. Like Novak Djokovic at 36, they need inner mental strength and strong legs to play for a few more years.

Marriage is a charming and chaotic life at the same time. The name of the game is adjustment. Ignoring, bouncing back with a smile after being pulverised, and striving to strengthen weak vibes, are ways to ensure marriage works.

It's about making smart moves like in a chess game. It is a gargantuan feat; a long journey with many ups and downs, twists and turns.

Enjoy the journey. Bear in mind that your kids are watching your verbal *dangals,* which can have a bearing later on in their life. You can make your marriage a *gulistan* by letting the barbs slide and having a big heart.

I overheard a conversation between two mid-aged men seemingly leading a happy life at a convenience store. *'Bazurrg keh gaye hain ki agar khush rehna hai to shaadi mat karo!* I was surprised. Their next pearl of wisdom, *'Shaadi woh laddoo hai jo khaaye bhi pachtaye aur na khaaye bhi pachtaye.'*

Why did these wise men marry themselves? Their life would or could have become hell, especially in old age.

'Har kisi ko mukkamal jahan nahin milta.' Likewise, no one gets an ideal life partner. The only way out of a rotten relationship is divorce, which is another big, expensive, emotionally tiring hassle.

My take—be happy with what you have. *Khush raho* because happiness is a choice. The alternative could be worse. *Dur ke dhol hamesha suhaane lagte hain.*

Why do Ladies Go to the House of God?

This is a true story enacted in quite a few gurdwaras and mandirs. About ten ladies of a colony used to meet at the gurdwara at eight am every morning to hear the *katha*. One day, one of them got late. Her friends could not concentrate on the *katha* and the *shabads* the poor *granthi* was reciting. They were more worried about the absence of their friend. She finally came in at 9:30 am. It was with great difficulty that the friends spent the remaining thirty minutes till the *ardaas* were performed.

'Why did you come late today, *behna?*' asked all in chorus.

'Please tell me what was said in the *katha* first. After that, I will narrate an exciting fight in my neighbour's house.'

The friends finished the gist of the *katha* in three minutes flat and implored their friend

to narrate the fight. The lady described in great detail how she had to eavesdrop at the neighbour's door to get the details. More than forty-five minutes were spent analysing the fight.

Friends, exceptions can be there, but this is the usual practice followed in most places of worship. These houses of god have become places for rendezvous, gossip, backbiting, bickering, politics, ogling, and finding matches for children. I have encountered quite a few meetings between parents at Bangla Sahib Gurdwara in Delhi. If the prospective bride or bridegroom is acceptable, the elation is visible. If the candidate or 'commodity' is unacceptable, folks do not wait for a minute to discuss the minus points in the house of god itself. *'Kudi da kad chota siga! O chuhi Jai di lagdi si, umar 24 nahin, 27 lagdi si, kudi di maa bahut hi moti sigi.'* (The girl was short. She seemed to look twenty-seven years old instead of twenty-four. The girl's mother was obese.) Such exercises make one wonder if God exists, and if he does, he ought to punish such people.

Another fad is the clamour for the position of president and secretary. My colony has about 150 houses, and I gathered that there were 4-5 candidates for each post in the gurdwara election. And mind you, Sikh families would be hardly 20 percent in our colony. I can only say that it gives one's ego a high, and your status in your community goes northwards. Besides, you control funds that come as *charawa* and are engaged in conducting religious events. Do these worthy people think that God will be happy with their acts?

My take is that one should go to places of worship, but one should go to orphanages more. One should offer food and tea at gurdwaras and mandirs, but offering it to needy people will be far better. Mandirs and gurdwaras need to spend money on education and health. I hate to say it, but the majority of the Sikh clergy is illiterate. If they were to compete with the priests of churches, they would be no match. Universities in Punjab need to start courses in theology to train their clergy about religion, and theologists from other faiths need to be on the faculty to widen the horizons of the *granthis.* Often, a *granthi* can recite the Granthi Sahib (the holy book of Sikhs) by rote, but can he explain the meaning to a layperson?

I suggest the Guru Granthi Sahib be in English because that is the universal language. Otherwise, the Sikh religion stands the risk of vanishing. If you think about it rationally, can you possibly learn physics or math in Punjabi? I have grave doubts. We need to communicate and propagate in a language others can easily understand.

Accidental Moms

Dr Manmohan Singh was an Accidental PM. I am an accidental author. Quite a few girls become accidental mothers. The number shot up during Covid. I know two girls who did not want to attain motherhood, but they are very happy now. It is bliss but with a cost.

Welcome to the world of accidental mothers. Times have changed in India now. During our time, parents wanted to get their kids married as soon as possible and get into parenthood then. They felt that their responsibility was over. It is no longer so now. The girls are more interested in their careers than marriage. They prefer to marry a boy they know whose mental calibre and financial status matches theirs, if not better.

Kids today are more aware of the difficulties, oops, challenges of taking up this task. They know they may have to give up their lucrative jobs, get less time to travel and enjoy during the initial years, bother about school admissions, compromise independence by staying with in-laws or depend on helpers.

Becoming a mother is like climbing Mount Everest. I will term it as extremely painful happiness. You have to weigh the pros and cons. It is a Hamlet-like to-be-or-not-to-be situation. Bold girls prefer to be single as they do not find suitable matches. Others like Sushmita Sen are happy by adopting children.

Which category are you in, my dear kids? Opinions from parents are welcome.

Beauty, Paint, and Powder!

The immortal lines from this old song hold true even today. Women, especially ones above 50, give a lot of time to decking up. I have encountered couples who miss the *laavan pheres* of their friends' kids because the wives did not get ready in time.

My personal take; down-to-earth intelligent ladies with natural beauty and tranquillity, like Kashmir or Venice, are far better than the paint and powder ones. They have an all-around charm pleasing to the eye and exude warmth and innocence like kids. They touch your soul. They are witty, cool, and simple. Every time you meet them becomes memorable. They are really beautiful.

You do not have to flaunt your fake beauty and hit sixes all around in the social circuit like Shubam Gill is hitting, oops, was hitting in the IPL. You do not have to go in *lambi gaadis* and *mehngi saaris* for functions because it is difficult to meander through the awful roads of Delhi. You will take time to make the saree better than the best by tying it many times over and end up being late for the function.

True beauty comes with deeds, respecting people and not looking down on the have-nots. Only then will you gain genuine respect, not *nakli* respect. Do not burn out your skin and life. *Yeh bari keemti cheezen hain.* Ultimately your good deeds will talk.

On a lighter note, *gori ladkion ko nazar zyada lagti hai. Gorion ke divorce rate zyada hote hain kyon ki unki bari ego hoti hai.* Truly beautiful are the ones *jinka dil saaf hota hai aur bara hota hai.* They share their happiness. They spread *khushi* all around.

Become beautiful by your *karm.*

Chicken-hearted Cricketers, Actors, and Lioness Wrestlers!

There is no dearth of gutless wonders in India. They thrive in cricket and films. Their clownish acrobatic antics on the field or the screen would make them seem like Pathans. In actuality, they are far from it. Name, fame and money make them jump around like clowns and the public laps it all up. People are willing to brave the rain till 1:30 am for an IPL final as it gives them the thrills. A single movie can garner 1000 crores. But when it comes to real life, all goes silent. It's *chuppi.*

Except for Kapil Dev, Anil Kumble, Navjote Singh Sidhu, and Harbhajan Singh, the other demigod cricketers have adopted a *maun vrat* with regard to the protesting wrestlers' issue. *Sannata,* akin to a cremation ground, has engulfed tinseltown. I think they have a lot to lose. *Kuch sharam karo, nakli heroes.* Learn from Abhinav Bindra, Neeraj Chopra. and the millions of Indians who have got behind the just cause of the wrestlers.

The World Wrestling body has strongly condemned the action of Delhi Police when they bashed up the protesting wrestlers. Sakshi Malik, Vinita Phogat, and Babita Phogat have Jaat genes and are born fighters. They have won tough fights against world-class wrestlers at the Olympics, Asian Games, and Commonwealth Games. They will fight this battle of honour too till the end and win. They are the real heroines and are getting more and more support every day. It is a tough battle, but the girls are tough too. They seem to be made of steel and have very strong willpower.

The girls are setting an example for the Indians. If the ones who have got so many laurels for the country are having such a tough time, what will be the fate of the common person? It could be your child tomorrow! You will surely fight back as these brave girls are doing. Please support them.

PART III

Ducked a Bribe in Delhi and Stunned by Japanese Honesty

The year 1982 was the first time I was going to fly overseas. I believe the policeman at the entry gate of the international airport could see it all written on my face. He mistook me for a Punjabi Jat, boot illiterate Singh, on a maiden foreign jaunt.

'*O Sardara, kithe jaa reya hai?*'

'Japan.' He was nonplussed and made a funny face.

'*Othe ki kam karn jaa reya yan* (for what are you going there?)'

'*Apni company de kam vaaste jaa raya hon* (I am going for my company's work),' I responded.

He had expected me to be a passenger for UK or USA and could not fathom what I would do in Japan.

'*Mainu 50 rupaye de* (give me 50 rupees),' he asked as a matter of right.

'*Mere kol change nahi hegi* (I don't have change),' I replied.

'*Mere kol hege ya* (I have change),' he responded with alacrity. He took out a 50-rupee note and thrust it into my hand.

'*Mainu hun 100 rupaye de* (you give me the 100 rupees).'

I was in a playful mood. I took the Rs. 50 note and walked past him, I wanted to teach him a lesson. He was stunned.

'*Sardarji, eki* (Mr Singh, what is this)?'

'*Main nahin denda tenu* (I will not give the money),' I responded, pushing my baggage trolley towards the immigration counter. He pleaded, he begged.

'*Sir, mere paise tan mod dao* (Sir, please return my money).'

I had no intention of running away with his money, but I wanted him to remember me for the rest of his life. I am sure he did. If he could do it with me, I am sure he was doing it with others also.

The moment I entered the JAL aircraft, I thought I had been transported to a different world. The air hostesses greeted each passenger like a VIP. The plane was clinically clean. The services were excellent. I was awed by the long lines at the immigration counter at Narita.

It did not take me more than fifteen minutes to clear the customs. The smart young lady saw my face and passport and said, 'Welcome to Japan, Singh San.' The ride to my hotel was heavenly. I still remember the trees on the side of the road and the wide, spotlessly clean road on which the bus glided smoothly.

The instructions given to me by my first Japanese boss were very simple. I got down at the Tokyo station and took a cab for a short ride to my hotel, which was near my office. It was a small cosy joint, and I was bowled over by my room which was very small but had all the amenities in perfect order. I got up early and decided to go for a walk in the vicinity of the hotel. I found people literally running. I was foxed; my colleague told me later that they were running to reach the office before time so that they could start their day on a winning note.

I was treated like a Prince by the steel department. Quite a few Japanese who were not well-versed about India were amused at my turban. They thought I was Iranian or Afghani. My schedule had been arranged with clockwork precision, where I met the team members of different departments and was taken to the plants with which I was developing business. We rarely had to take a taxi, and that too for a short distance from the metro to the client's office. I was taken to different Japanese restaurants every evening and had the opportunity of tasting beef for the first and the last time in my life because I could not say no to the GM of the division who was hosting me.

But what will remain permanently etched in my memory is an incident that happened on my last day in Tokyo. I had an extensive shopping list, got many things for my family and friends, and was helped by a Japanese colleague who had spent practically the whole Saturday with me. He left me at the station, as I could reach my hotel alone by cab. When the cab reached the hotel, I settled the bill with the driver, sitting in the front seat, as my shopping bags took the space behind. The cab whizzed past the red light and I realised my folly the moment I entered the lobby. I was empty-handed as I had foolishly forgotten all my bags in the cab. I panicked and started sweating for fear of creating a wrong impression. I did not dare call up my colleagues, who would have thought me thoroughly irresponsible. I visualised the sneers I would get from my family when I told them of my faux pas. I sat down in the lobby like a shattered, crumpled flower.

The guest relations lady in the lobby sensed something was wrong, 'Singh San, how was your day?'

'The day was good, but it ended on a sad note,' I replied in a shattered voice.

'Why? What happened?' she inquired with concern.

'Like a bloody fool, I forgot to pick up my shopping bags when I got out of the taxi. It was the only shopping I had done, and there were about ten bags,' I responded with a tearful face.

'Oh! She was genuinely concerned. Don't worry; we will do something to retrieve your bags,' she reassured me.

'How can you? I don't have the cab number.'

'Don't worry,' she replied. 'Please go to your room and rest.'

It was nine pm. How could they trace my bags without a clue? I did not have dinner, packed my suitcase, and lay on the small bed with open eyes, sleep having vanished, waiting for the long torturous night to end.

Miracles happen, and honesty does exist in this world. My hotel started making calls to the taxi companies and gave my description and the shopping bags mistakenly left by me in one cab. I am sure many people must have gotten involved, but around midnight, I got a call from the receptionist who first apologised for disturbing me and then shared the good news that my bags had been found. The driver of the cab was waiting at the reception with my bags. I hugged him. He was confused but could well understand my emotional outburst. I was delighted. I took out a $100 bill and gave it to the driver. He returned the bill and told the receptionist to inform me in English that he was just doing his duty and wanted me to leave his country with a good impression. There were tears in my eyes.

Networking!

Branding is delivery, satisfaction, and trust. Brands are able to get a good following because of these main factors. Coco-Cola, Pepsi, and Amitabh Bachchan are favourable brands because people believe in them. Amitabh Bachchan is an icon because he is the favourite of all age groups, whereas the youth prefers Pepsi. Nirma created a brand for itself because it delivered to a different segment. They are giving Hindustan Lever a run for their money.

I was a rookie in the business field. Networking was my forte, and I learnt this art from my father. It helped me a lot at Itochu Corporation. I could arrange meetings for my bosses and senior functionaries from Itochu overseas offices as I had kept in touch with my friend's seniors and juniors from school and college. The biggest mistake people make is that they are reminded of their alma mater only when the time for admission of their children comes. They could go places and help you when you need them. Please keep in touch with them, call them, and meet them, even for a while.

Thanks to my networking skills, I got opportunities with CEOs of big companies, senior bureaucrats sitting in prestigious positions and cabinet members. They had good words to say about me and went out of their way to help me develop good business.

Do not remain confined to only one field. I saw most people sticking to their divisions during my visit to companies and even at Itochu Corporation. If he were handling machinery, he would stick to it for an entire lifetime. I seized the initiative to request my management to allow me to handle various items simultaneously. This opened my business horizons and made me meet experts in various fields. I was inquisitive about products and projects, and the experts were happy to help me.

I was fortunate to create a personal brand for myself when I was given the GM Strategic Business Development position at Itochu Corporation. I strongly believe in the three Rs formula—Respect yourself, Respect for others, and taking Responsibility for all my actions. My trump card was relations.

I seized the initiative to take up more work than was given to me and was curious to learn new things. When I realised I had made mistakes, I was willing to take responsibility and strive to correct them.

I knew that success would come after many efforts, and I succeeded in catching the eye of the head office. I dared to learn and learnt to dare during my innings with the Japanese.

I painted the best picture of myself. The Japanese found an air of cockiness about me, but I had built my confidence level through preparation.

Imagine it, try it, and prove it by doing. I realised early in life that there is no express elevator to success. You have to take the stairs. No one will help you if you are incapable of helping yourself. I used to seize the initiative to learn about new things and managed to handle various products simultaneously. I had courage, conviction, and the urge to learn.

I thought differently; hence I felt differently and behaved differently, and ultimately achieved differently. The Japanese appreciated these traits in me and gave me plenty of opportunities to flourish. The main difference between the people who succeed in life and those who fail in life is a single word—initiative. I had it in plenty. I took more than what was on my plate. I requested my bosses to send me overseas to develop business, and they rarely said no. I am a full-time optimist by nature. When I went to meetings, I went with the intent of winning.

Strive and Thrive: We Have Much to Learn from the Japanese

'Your country has abundant natural resources. I am quite surprised that you are still not self-sufficient.' The venerable Japanese sitting next to me on the flight to Tokyo seemed to know more about India than most Indians do.

'You are right, but whereas your countrymen strive for excellence, most of us struggle for survival,' was my weak defensive reply.

'Have you ever in your life been without shoes?' he asked me suddenly. I took his statement as an affront and was quick to react.

'I have never been through such dire straits. I may not be wealthy, but life has treated me well.'

'It has been more than fifty years, but I still remember the terrible times we went through after Japan was razed to the ground in 1945. I was barely twelve and vividly remember walking barefoot to school in the biting cold. My mother had only one change of clothes. About twenty families used to share a common toilet cum bathroom. I will never forget that winter of 1945. If we could do it, why can't you?' His Kennedy-like rhetorical statement set me pondering.

Japan is smaller than Madhya Pradesh, and its population is less than Uttar Pradesh. It completely depends on imports of essential minerals like iron ore, gas, coats, and quite a few other items. In spite of these handicaps, Japan is amongst the top industrial powers in the world. It imports iron ore from countries like India and sells the finished steel back to these countries at competitive prices.

I got an opportunity to visit the Mitsubishi Steel Plant in Japan many years ago. I was floored by the cleanliness standards. The entrance seemed like some national park. I still recall that this plant produced about three million tons of steel yearly, with a workforce of fewer than five thousand. Practically everything was computerised; I juxtaposed it with the Bhilai Steel Plant, which produced less than 1 million tons and had a workforce of about 90,000.

Comparisons are odious, but my personal opinion is that the concept of public sector should be done away with now in India as it is the time of the survival of the fittest. If you cannot compete, you will perish.

I travelled by Air India recently and saw the dramatic difference since the Tatas have taken over. It was world-class service. Deja vu, Japanese style. I was very happy.

I am sure the earlier government serving-lackadaisical staff and ostrich-type attitude management has finally realised that they are in the service industry. They seemed to be under the illusion that they were on a paid holiday and stood the risk of being wiped out. Tatas will surely turn Air India around.

Having worked with the Japanese for about three decades, I can state with conviction that we Indians are as intelligent, if not more, than the Japanese. However, there are traits which we Indians need to emulate.

- Teamwork
- Sense of accountability and responsibility
- Dedication
- Loyalty

We Indians have a crab-like attitude and tend to waste more time denigrating others than trying to improve ourselves. Maybe it is the hot weather, but as a rule, we are averse to hard work.

Infosys, Tatas, J. K, Wipro, Mahindra and other Indian success stories prove India is best positioned for talented people. We should take the cue from the Japanese working style, or we may prove right poet Iqbal's immoral lines right once again.

'Na samjho ge to mit jaao ge e Hidustan vaali,
Tumhari dastan tak bhi na hogi daastanon mein.'

Winning, a Way of Life

'Motivation is what gets you started. Habit is what keeps you going.'

—Anonymous.

1. *Ganbaru* means stubbornly persevering and slogging on tenaciously. It is a Japanese word that means doing more than one's best.
2. *Erflog,* in German, means success.
3. *Haathon ki lakiren se zindagi nahin banti azam hamara bhi hissa hai, apna zindagi banana ka* (you can make your own destiny).
4. Bouncing back very fast from adversity
5. Networking skills
6. Fitness (mental and physical)
7. Humility
8. Focus
9. Deadline and goal

In a seesaw battle between the mind and body, the Japanese beat the mental tape. They are quick learners and always focus on the big picture. The advantages they have are humility and discipline. They will never be late for meetings. They are mission-oriented, unfailingly cheerful when they want to be cheerful and take maximum advantage of unity.

Prime Minister Narendra Modi has a keen desire to make India a developed country. Japan was the first country he visited when he took over the reins of the administration. The ease of doing business has improved, but we are still far behind countries like Singapore, where you can form a company in one day. We may not catch up with Japan and the other nations, but we can take some positive steps in the right direction.

Mr. Modi can start the cleanliness drive, but our citizens must take the initiative to clean up the environment. In my extensive travel overseas, the only country which matched India in the dirt was the Yemen Arab Republic. India will have to learn to keep their environment clean. Why is it that Indians keep their own houses clean but tend to throw litter on the street roads openly? Why do Indians follow their best practices overseas but forget the same in their country? The only place in India I found clean was Indore (Madhya Pradesh). If they could do it, other cities need to replicate their best practices.

Corona has played havoc with the world and India. But you still find people roaming around without masks, flouting the law blatantly. Motor accidents don't occur in Japan, but if they do, the errant motorists do not adopt the hit-and-run tactics. A friend told me about an incident in Tokyo when a girl hit a person in her speeding car and fled away. The girl's father took her to the police station and asked them to take necessary action. He was also willing to pay the hospital expenses of the victim. Would that happen in India? No way.

The errant driver will speed away, oblivious to the injuries that he has caused to the victim.

In other countries, people pay taxes. In India, less than five percent of the population does so. The government needs to take stringent action against evaders by putting heavy penalties.

Women can walk without fear, even at midnight in Tokyo. My friend Srikanth who lived in Tokyo for three years from 1967-1970, told me that he and his mother could walk alone at night without any problem. It is not the same in the capital of Delhi even today. People are afraid to venture out at night for fear of being robbed. People are robbed in daylight too.

Japanese exude humility. They are politeness personified. Indians tend to flaunt their wealth. Japanese take out their cars only on the weekends. Indians have a weakness for showing off their big cars on narrow roads, and sometimes one person has more than one car for which there is no necessity. Japanese have simple weddings, and the number of guests is limited. Indians have lavish weddings. In Japan, the bride and bridegroom arrange their weddings. In India, preparations start six months in advance, and parents take over the arrangement of several ceremonies. Precious food is wasted.

In Japan and other countries, you are an adult at eighteen and tend to move out. You visit your parents during Christmas holidays or special occasions. In India, you are a child even when you turn sixty. Parents save money for their children, buy plots and the fixed deposit in their name, oblivious of their own well-being.

There are no strikes in Japan. In India, they are the norm. People are least bothered about holding up traffic but do not realise they are taking the country backwards. The Japanese combine passion with compassion, truthfulness with trust, and persistence with resistance to temptations. They are nationalistic and the biggest brand ambassadors for their country when they go overseas. This is very unlike Indians, who find fault with everything around them. Surprisingly, when the same Indians settle overseas, they yearn for India and miss its pluses.

The Japanese have mastered the just-in-time management philosophy. Their production and delivery are always on time. India is catching up to some extent, but there is room for

improvement. Japanese are quiet, and Indians are loud. Japanese keep their head to the ground, and most Indians have a head-in-the-air demeanour. Japan is a small country smaller than Madhya Pradesh, but they have cracked the formula that makes them tick. They strive to better their performances.

Japanese are passionate about their work. Majority of Indians are lackadaisical. For the Japanese, work and worship are two sides of the same coin. They have moved from their area of weakness to areas of strength. We are still struggling. Time is neutral. It is neither anybody's friend nor enemy. Japanese know to value time. We still have a long way to go.

Japanese use their words very carefully. They think twice before talking. We are slippery without realising that one wrong word can destroy your life. Japanese do not become victims. They accept responsibility for their actions. We indulge in finding scapegoats. A typical example of an Indian parent is when his child topples a chair and starts howling, the indignant parent kicks the chair. The child starts thinking, 'I am not responsible.' He will turn out to be an irresponsible adult.

Winning and losing is all in your hands. As Winston Churchill said, 'Never, never give up.' The Japanese follow the same principle. Most Indians tend to give up even before they start the battle for life.

When I used to go for overseas business, I had to sell my country first, then my product. No problem seems to be the biggest problem with most of the Indians. Improvement is there, but more needs to be done.

The Japanese infused some winning traits in me. They inculcated certain habits which have stood in good stead for a lifetime. They are; discipline, time management, reaching appointments well on time, going prepared for meetings, and talking less.

The Japanese are ingrained to work very hard. Most were smart, shrewd, remained tight-lipped, and opened their mouths only when necessary.

Their habit of having weekly meetings and sharing their progress with their entire staff was in the company's interest. They taught me to listen twice as much as I spoke. The reason for their success is positioning. They have made success a way of life. Japanese do not flirt with time. They value it.

Grabbing Opportunities

Japanese management collates in fine-tuning, shifting shaft from the grain, and defining data.

My Japanese bosses made me implement my ideas with precision, zeal, and dedication. They taught me that returns are poor when great ideas are implemented half-heartedly.

According to Dr. Philip Kotler, there are four Ps of success—produce, price, promotion, and people. Business is all about people. I was extremely fortunate to get the right people to work with. You have a better chance of selling your product if the people you are selling your products to like you.

I strengthened my relations by building bonds with my clients outside office. I would go to their houses and their functions. The Japanese gave me the experience of experiences. They taught me a precious lesson, i.e., there is only one thing more painful than learning from experience, and that is not learning from experience.

Napoleon Bonaparte said, 'Don't give me good generals. Give me lucky generals.' I was lucky to get an opportunity to work with many ace Japanese and people from other nationalities during my stint with Itochu Corporation.

As a rule, the local staff remains stuck in one business only while working with Japanese companies. Destiny made me handle products and projects and various products that I could develop and materialise business with many companies. Starting with steel imports and chrome

ore exports, I moved on to imports of paper, exporting to South Africa and the Middle East and imports from Japan. I also handled the tin cans export to the Middle East, apple imports from New Zealand, domestic flour and wheat flour, rice exports, and dairy products business.

Sports and Business

'If Rishi had his way, he would convert Itochu into a sports company,' said Yamamoto San when we met the Delhi Chief Minister Sheila Dikshit. When the worldwide Chairman of Itochu Corporation asked me during a meeting which business Itochu could develop for maximum leverage, I said, 'Sports Business.'

I gave a proposal to my management for hiring the boxer Yogendra Singh who had won the bronze medal at the Beijing Olympics, to promote our food brand. Vijendra had bagged a contract with Pepsi for Rs. 1 crore and Bajaj Alliance for Rs. 25 lakhs. Due to our unique relations with Vijendra's agent, we succeeded in bringing down the price from Rs. 50 Lakhs to Rs. 25 lakhs.

Itochu preferred to give a famous film star Rs. 1 crore but did not consider my request. They would surely have received excellent returns on investment from Vijendra as they did from the famous actor.

There is a correlation between business and sports. Both involve teams setting targets, monitoring progress, and achieving goals. Just as sports is the perfect training ground for success, so is doing business. My involvement in sports helped me develop leadership skills like self-disciple and morale building. It helped me strive for higher goals and move with winners so that I could imbibe the best qualities from them.

Harvard Business School surveyed about 40 alumni who became business CEOs. All the respondents reported playing some games during their growing up. My alma mater St. Stephen's College, Delhi, inculcated in me an interest in sports. This helped me throughout my life. I took up race walking and cross country as my events. I fell unconscious in my first year during the inter-college championships. In the second year, I came third, and in the third year, I came second. Sports taught me to win and lose business in my stride and hence taught me to handle my business better.

I kept in touch with my sporting friends, and quite a few of them became senior bureaucrats and CEOs of big companies. It was easier for me to get through to them to facilitate the Itochu business. These friends were cool in college; they were cool even later. They did not let failure let them down in college. It was déjà vu now too.

The irony of Indians is that we have more hospitals than playgrounds. I can guarantee that if we make more playgrounds, the hospital business will feel threatened. If you are a sports person, your hospital bills for visits to doctors and hospitals will automatically decline. You will perform better. Japanese are engaged in individual and team sports, so they are fit. They play golf and football during their posting in India.

Institutes and companies are not made of four walls. It is the students and staff that make these companies great. Students from the best institutes get jobs in the best companies. Japanese staff sent to India are normally sent to learn the ropes to get proficient clients.

Team sports involve scoring goals. The Japanese taught me the art of scoring winning goals. You have to pay the price for success. I learnt from the Japanese that they have paid a heavy price for making Japan what it is today. They do not give up. They failed multiple times before hitting their bull's-eye. They are winners.

Mohammed Ali, the famous boxer, said more than half a century ago, 'Winners are not made in gyms. They are made from something that comes from deep within a dream, a desire, and a vision. They have to have the last-minute stamina, they have to be a little faster, they have

to have the skill and the will, but the will must be stronger than the skill.'

Japan succeeded because it had the inner desire and will to succeed.

How Can Japanese Companies Get More out of Their Indian Staff?

Though they may have the commonality of Buddhism, the tyranny of distance, the language, the food, and the culture makes it challenging for Indians and Japanese to be in sync. I will twist Pakistan's founder Mohammad Ali Jinnah's statement on the foundation of Pakistan that 'Pakistan can do without America, but America cannot do without Pakistan because of its strategic location.' I will say that India can do without Japan, but Japan cannot do without India. And, for the good of both, it is best to co-exist collectively, collaborate and strengthen the relations.

In Japanese trading companies in India, a Japanese boss, as an expert, comes for tenure of about three years. He gets a cultural shock when he lands in India because of the number of people and the chaotic atmosphere. Even though he has learnt to speak English, in case he has not stayed in the US, he finds it difficult to understand people with different speaking styles. Having spent most of his life travelling long distances in Tokyo by train while going to and fro from office and home, a Mercedes with a dedicated chauffeur 24x7 is a luxury he is not prepared for. Habitual of staying in compact houses in Japan, he is overwhelmed by the size of the apartments he is allotted along with the paraphernalia of cooks, maids, cleaners etc. His family is more awed.

In normal circumstances, he takes about six months to acclimatise to his surroundings and the business he has been entrusted to overlook. Ironically, his subordinate has much more experience than he has and has the added advantage of being on his own turf. If there is a matching of minds, the innings of both the boss and subordinate are smooth, but in actuality, it is a rarity.

For the Indian staff, it is like a new marriage after every three years. He has to learn to adjust to the whims and fancies of his boss. There are instances when young Japanese bosses who have hardly spent 5-10 years in Tokyo headquarters are lording over subordinates who have spent three decades in the organisation.

Even though the prime aim of the Japanese expert is business, he is caught in the vortex of the Japanese social and golf circuit, leaving him with insufficient time to share his expertise with his subordinates or develop a new business and take it to the final stage. It is good luck if it is an ongoing business, but if he is entrusted with developing a business from scratch, it is quite a monumental task.

The Japanese business veterans who have had stints in various offices overseas find adjusting to their new business environment much easier because they understand that business takes time. Still, quite a few youngsters are in a hurry to achieve results to impress the CEO, and the divisions that have sponsored them make life very difficult for the Indian staff and themselves.

Japanese trading houses should seriously start emulating American and European companies that entrust the top job to capable Indians after training them for the same. I can guarantee that the results will be far better because the Indian CEO understands the environment better than the Japanese and will go the extra mile to forge the Japanese management's faith in him.

The salary structure in several Japanese companies is not what it should be. This leads to a quick attrition rate for young recruits who enter the company with many expectations, which are belied when they see the reality. After a year or two, they seek greener pastures and move on. The staff working for two to three decades is the biggest sufferer. They have gotten used to the company's ways and given their sweat, blood, and tears to raise it from the base to the present stage. They feel lost when they are bypassed for promotions or are ill-treated by their Japanese bosses. The wise amongst them start preparing themselves while in service to chalk out a career for themselves, and some are lucky to retain the manufacturers who prefer to work with them instead of the company because they charge less commission and know the business like the back of their hand. The worst are the oldies that have nowhere to go and are stuck. They take the hits and volleys with a smile on their face and a tear in their hearts.

Indians, too, need to move on from their self-centred stance to a more team-building approach where they need to take each boss as a captain and strive to play their parts to the hilt. In my experience at Itochu Corporation, I have encountered several spoilsport Indians who, for their selfish interests, portray themselves as holier than the Pope to the Japanese staff and create a rift between the bosses and subordinates.

Sometimes drivers, too, can be Machiavellian in their approach. I will never forget the sporty gesture of the last CEO; I worked under Mr. H. Shimuzu at Itochu India. Despite his admin staff advising him that I was not entitled to my LTC and lose one month's leaving notice, he went ahead and gave me both. It was a magnanimous gesture, which will make me respect him for years to come. The gesture by the local staff to score brownie points will make me obliterate him from my list of contacts.

Many years ago, I encountered a driver who added fuel to the fire raging between me and my Japanese boss in the early 90s. The driver took up the role of James Bond and used to inform my boss of my movements even in my absence, hoping against hope that his godfather could get him the seat I was holding. He went on overdrive and made up false accusations that I abused the boss in Punjabi behind his back and that I was spending far too much time for my meeting.

Eventually, nothing happened. I shifted to a new division, the Japanese boss returned, and the driver left the company after a few years as he could not get the royal treatment he was getting from his next boss. But he did wrangle several electronic items and household goods free of cost from his benefactor when his departure came.

Veg in India, Non-Veg Overseas

I came across various strange double-faced Indian business folks during the course of my work. One such was AS. He had business in his blood and lived in a joint family with his parents, brothers, and a comely wife.

I developed a product with him that I found extremely interesting, but I found AS more interesting than the product we were developing. I met his family during my visits to his house and at the various social functions he arranged.

The family was pure *vaishnu,* i.e., totally vegetarian. They would not touch non-vegetarian food or alcohol. The patriarch who had started the business in the early 50s was like a field marshal, and all his sons bowed to his diktat.

They say you come to know a man when you travel with him. Many years ago, we visited Japan to meet the manufacturers and the Itochu Corporation head office team handling that product. It was a bit of a shock for me when I saw AS ordering whiskey and non-veg snacks the moment the staff started serving on the flight. The look on my face told him that I was taken off guard.

'Bhai Saab jab Hindustan ki sarhad ke bahar hote hain, iske bare mein muhn pe tala laga leejiye please. Yeh raaz

raaz he rahega agar tum kisi se kuch na kaho.' I suppressed a smile.

I was in for more surprises when we checked into our hotel in Tokyo. We had our meeting the next day, but our friend was in a horny mood. Just as drunkards and card players can find others like them very easily, so can people who want to have a good time away from home. He asked the receptionist where the red light district was and whether it could be reached by a direct metro. The receptionist smiled and wrote the directions and the place's name on a piece of paper.

'I am sure you are joining me, Rishi.'

'Yes, Bhai Saab, I am, but I am afraid I do not have the guts.'

'Come, come, I will put the guts in you.'

'You seem to be an experienced player in this field,' I asked innocently.

'Yaa, I do not miss the opportunity whenever I am overseas.'

Night had fallen; we reached the destination, looked at 3-4 establishments, and decided on one.

'Let's conquer Tokyo on our first night,' he said in glee, 'And as it is your first experience outside marriage, let it be a treat from my side.'

It took me a lot of time to reinforce my dissent, but my playful mode came to the fore just as he entered the field for his match.

'Bhai Saab, I was just wondering that, just in case, while you are having fun with a sexy girl, you have a heart attack in excitement, what should I do?'

'*Hare Ram, Hare Ram, Rishi aisi baaten mat kiya karo.* You should wish me luck, and I will narrate my experience while you do window shopping.'

He emerged after about one hour like a warrior who had succeeded in a battle. '*Mazaa aa gaya.*'

'How much did this bliss cost you?'

'About $100, but while I was enjoying, I wondered whether it would have been more appropriate to spend the amount for my kids or my wife.'

I could not understand the twisted thoughts as we walked towards the metro station to rest and recharge ourselves for a hectic week ahead.

Locked in a Train Toilet

I was going to Ludhiana with my boss, Yama San, for a meeting and had a forgettable experience.

I am sure quite a few people have had the experience of being locked in toilets at home and office but have weathered the storm. A few years ago, I had a harrowing time after getting locked inside the toilet of a moving train. Besides quite a few missed heartbeats, I became the butt of jokes of the entire compartment of the Rajdhani Express.

I had gone for a piddle, and after satisfactory relieving and washing my hands, I tried to pull up the latch to open the door. The blasted thing would not open. I tried once, twice and then a couple of times without success. Slight beads of sweat crept on my forehead and chest. What if I got locked in? Left with no options, I started knocking softly at the door and then with all my vigour.

'Kholo, kholo.' For a few minutes, there was no response. My heartbeat became faster. What if I had a heart attack? 'What if' and a thousand negative thoughts crossed my mind in a few moments.

I heaved a sigh of relief when I heard a voice at the other end. *'Kee hoya?'*

'Mera darwaza lock ho gaya ya, ainu please kholo.' The good man outside made a sincere effort but failed. He assured me that he would bring help. He brought five other men who tried with all their might but failed.

'Sir, you must find a technician who can take me out. Can you please request the coach attendant?'

'Okay, we will.'

I had been inside my moving jail for over half an hour, and it seemed like the longest thirty minutes of my life.

After about twenty minutes, the voice at the other end of the technician was like Mozart's voice to my ears. I came out of the toilet shaken, stirred, rattled and embarrassed. My experience had the ears of the entire compartment, who looked at me with funny, pitiable eyes.

However, the last word went to my father, who regaled everyone with the one-liner, *'Bechare Sardar sahib toilet vich phas gaye siye.'* I certainly did not find it funny, but I witnessed quite a few mirthful eyes whenever I crossed the passageway.

Yama San—My Best Japanese Boss

He was sent by God to improve me. He was as silent as an iceberg and had a Socrates-type approach. He believed in the philosophy that life is not about scoring goals but playing well and with passion. Goals would automatically be achieved. Working under him was enlightening, enriching, and an enervating experience.

He was one of Itochu's treasures brought to India by the Itochu India CEO after retirement because the latter had worked under him in his divisions. He took me under his wing, cared for me, and his advice gave me a lot of strength.

He gave me the sobriquet *Ritusopoi,* which means too argumentative. 'If you can control your tongue and think before hearing something, you can shape yourself as an excellent businessman.'

'My mother has been trying to put this pearl of wisdom into my head for many decades, and she has not succeeded. I sincerely hope you can,' I responded.

Yama San was gifted with a sixth sense. Like most of his countrymen, he had tremendous faith in intuition. He could tell whether a business had potential or not, and he would set a timeline for the result or to close the file for the same.

He instilled in me the gambit trait, which means working very hard and seemed to have the energy and the age of a twenty-year-old at sixty-five. His unfiltered feedback, unlike filtered coffees, was the foodstuff I got in the mornings.

We developed business from Amritsar to Tamil Nadu and handled various products. He was truly touched visiting the Vatican of the Sikhs, the Golden Temple in Amritsar during one of our visits there. I got the following business sermons from Yama San.

1. Read and reread your emails/letters carefully.
2. Be humble.
3. Be gutsy when you know your subject. Say what you mean and mean what you say.
4. Keep professional and personal life separate.
5. To be a good leader, first become a good follower.
6. Avoid arguing, especially with your boss. You will always be the loser.
7. Do not teach the Bible to the Pope.

In 2008, the Food Conference was held in Shanghai, China. Yama San asked me to prepare a presentation for the same. We must have changed it ten times before he gave me the approval for my draft. A time came when I knew the presentation by heart, but he would not rest. Thirty-five representatives from other Itochu offices were giving their presentations, and he wanted my presentation to be the best. While waiting at the airport lounge, he repeatedly made me rehearse the presentation. 'Rishi, don't look at that girl. You can do all this after the presentation.'

I was fully prepared and charged for the presentation when D-day arrived. I started my presentation by making the participants laugh when I said, 'I belong to a tiny country on the world map called India, with a population of only one billion.' The presentation went very smoothly. There were a few questions which I answered confidently. I got a huge round of applause. Yama San got up from his seat and hugged me. 'Well done, Rishi.' This was unusual for a Japanese. I was thrilled.

I had one extra day with me and looked around Shanghai. It had changed a lot. When I went there for the first time in 1989, it was a little like Gurgaon, India. Now it matched the standards of Tokyo and New York.

In 1989 the infrastructure in China was good but not as good as in 2008. China held the 2008 Olympics, where they showcased to the world that they had arrived. In 1989, I had gone for chrome ore exports to Ching Ming and ore exports. I took a cab to the airport well within time. I never imagined that I would get caught in a traffic jam. Wonder of wonders I did, thanks to the Singapore PM's entourage. I panicked. The poor driver could not understand my language. I could not understand his. I could as well have talked in Punjabi.

I missed the flight to Hong Kong. I could not explain my plight to the counter girl. I wanted to talk to someone because I had no cell phone. I had spent all my money on buying gifts. I spent the night at the airport without having food and water. I was famished. Luckily I got a seat on the flight the next day. It was a memorable trip indeed.

I bid Yama San farewell at the India International Centre, Delhi. I invited my friends from the corporate world with whom we had done business. I also invited some top-notch bureaucrats. I gave a very passionate, emotional speech. 'It has been a privilege being the flock of my corporate shepherd, Yama San. He had been a mixture of the toughness of granite and softness of blossoms, sharp as a razor and coolness of a mountain stream. I have loved dancing the corporate tunes of Yama San. I want to tango with him in Spain and samba in Brazil later.' Artificial modesty did not suit me. Yama San brought me to the ground. I wish he had come into my life a little sooner.

Hirako San—Who Took the
Best out of Me

It was 12th April, 2004, at five pm in Hirako San's office. 'You have not been able to take full advantage of your capability and connections. You are good. You are still young and energetic and must show your talent to the new CEO Mr. Yamamoto. I will talk to him, but ultimately the decision lies with him.'

Having built faith in Hirako San, I had requested him to suggest to the new CEO to involve me in the business development strategy and let me play the role of Executive Assistant to the India CEO. The timing was perfect, and I succeeded. The next five years under the leadership of Yamamoto San were among the finest I had. Hirako San took me under his wing and brought about a phenomenal transformation in my personality. He made me work not hard but very hard with the intent of improving my performance.

'You have talent, and I have decided to put that talent to good use.' He gave me an opportunity to handle the oil, timber, and paper businesses at the same time. In addition, he asked me to give him weekly reports on India's political and economic situation. These opportunities opened my horizons. He would take me to meetings with the top business honchos of the country, which helped me pick up their traits.

He was blunt with me, pointed out my weaknesses, and expected me to overcome them and move from my areas of weakness to areas of strength. 'HP, you can have power only if you generate business, especially new business. Your problem is you are very proud. You should learn to be humble. You can improve only if you come down and be grounded. The timber business you have initiated is like a giant wheel. It takes time to start, but it will become a regular affair once it comes into motion. We need to energise business at the operational level. The three ingredients of success are patience, perseverance and humour.'

These pearls of wisdom were shared during car rides to meet clients, and these one-to-one meetings acted as boosters to me. He looked like a boxer; he was stocky and very quick on his feet. But most importantly, he had leadership qualities and, like an army commander, kept the India staff on its toes. He introduced weekly meetings where each department would share with the entire staff what they did, whom they met, and the business developed and finalised. We were a liaison office, and our funds used to come from the parent division of the head office. He trained the India staff to think on principal office lines and generate money from their own business. He was from the oil business division but during his tenure, he went into the minutest details of each business division and gave his ideas for taking the business to a higher level.

'I push you too hard. You must be tired.' I was sitting across the table from Hirako San, who was reviewing my report on the oil crisis implications for India. 'I do that to people I want to improve, and it is a good opportunity for you to handle the oil business, which has a great future in India. I admire you for your guts and your drive. You made a good report. I want a detailed study done, and I want you to start from the basics. It is good if you take 98 steps and take the right steps. But if you falter on the 99th step, you are finished.'

This was the blow-hot-blow-cold manner in which Hirako San honed my business skills, and I greatly improved. He used to load me with pearls of wisdom that always assumed that clients knew more than you. This was the fastest way to improve.

Ota San - The King Who Gave me Royal Rides in Business

He was my happiness-cum-business coach. Doing business with him gave me the Mt. Everest of happiness. It did not seem like I was doing business, but we did big business. He came into my life when I was around forty and he was around thirty.

He had mastered the six S's of life—strength, stamina, speed, skill, suppleness and spirit. He used them in the art of doing business and made it a sort of spiritual process.

What is spirituality? It can be bifurcated into two parts—spirit and vitality. Athletes like Roger Federer, P.V. Sindhu, and Virat Kohli are always in the zone. So was Ota San.

He visited India several times to develop business and invited me to Japan quite a few times. He also took me to France, Lithuania, Italy, Germany, and Holland to strike deals. Doing business with him was a pleasure indeed.

A funny incident happened during our trip to Lithuania. The connecting flight from Frankfurt was delayed, and my baggage did not reach me in time. As business schedules are very tight, I did not have time to buy another suit for my meeting. For the first time, I attended a business meeting in my tracksuit and jogging shoes, which I wear during long flights. We explained my lack of proper dressing to our hosts, and they fully understood.

Of his several trips to India, Ota San stayed at a hotel only for the first time. After that, he preferred to stay in my house and called my third-floor room, where he was put up, as President's Suites even though it just had a fan. Once when the electricity went off, he enjoyed the experience.

He loved Indian food and relished it during his India trip. He took me to many Indian and Japanese restaurants during my visits to Japan. I went to his house every time I was there, even for other businesses.

His wife Kumiko San and his daughter Shiori San treated me like a king. They invited the family of my friend, Harpreet, when he stopped in Japan on the way to Canada. Ota San did not know Harpreet, but he went out of his way to make him happy. A grand gesture of friendship indeed.

Why Are Foreigners Reluctant to Do Business with India?

A foreigner often gets a feel of the Indian system even before stepping out of the airport. The *thulla* (police constable) manning the immigration counter sizes up the half-asleep *murga* (bait), tired after a long flight and yearning to catch a few winks of sleep before starting a busy day.

'Your pen very nice. Can I have it?'

The poor first-timer to India is wide awake by now and rues when he placed his Montblanc in his coat pocket. He clutches his possession like a mother clutches her toddler from impending danger.

'Sorry, I have to use it,' he replies timidly.

'Then can I have US$5 *baksheesh*, Sir?'

'What is *baksheesh?*' the foreigner asks.

'It is a tip, Sir.' He parts with the money with a heavy heart and a silent curse on his lips.

This is the welcome that many outsiders used to get on landing in India, the land of opportunities, the country which, along with China, is rated by economists as the best hunting ground for business opportunities in the new millennium.

Why are foreigners wary of doing business with India? Why are small countries like Japan, Thailand, UAE, and Malaysia attracting more investors? India remains a poor hunting ground for overseas business despite its vast natural resources and an over-eager government willing to boost business.

Mr. Yoshinobu Ota, head of the dairy division of a leading Japanese company, was very enthusiastic about doing business with India. He negotiated with a premier Indian company engaged in the dairy business, cleared the samples of skimmed milk powder, visited the plant that matched his standards, settled the price, and signed a contract. He returned to Japan a happy and satisfied man. However, his happiness was short-lived because he received a terse note from the supplier a few days later that they could not hold on to the price. Poor Ota San was stunned. He had quoted for a big tender based on the offer, which was still valid. He caught the first available flight to India, but all his raving and ranting went to nought. He returned to Japan a dejected man. He lodged a complaint with the chairman of the company, who got to the bottom of the fiasco and found that an over-enthusiastic manager, in his zeal to get an entry into the Japanese market, had made a wrong calculation. But the damage had been done. Ota San lost his face. He shall think 100 times before doing business with India.

When I accompanied delegations abroad to sell Indian products, I noticed that we had to sell ourselves first, then our country, and finally our product. As a rule, foreigners are not keen on doing business with India. They find it extremely difficult to adjust to the unprofessional ethos of Indian business. Worse, if an order was placed for a particular item and the price fell, Indian businessmen would find some flaw to wriggle out of the contract. No problem seemed to be the biggest problem with Indian businessmen. Missing production deadlines, delaying LC openings and giving assurances of tomorrows that never came is a rule rather than an exception.

Strangely, Indians tend to perform better when they are outside India than when they are in India. I am sure the Silicon Valley air does not trigger the grey cells of the Indian millionaires who crop up every second day. Not that I am willing to believe that the 45-degree-plus climate of Dubai acts as a stimulant for Indians, who are, to a great extent, responsible for the growth of this once-upon-a-time desert land. Why is it that the culture of eating, chatting, and drinking tea is present in India's government offices only?

The three main elements lacking among us Indians are pride, discipline, and willpower. If we can cultivate these, we can easily project our country as the best possible place for doing business. We have a long way to go, but we must take the first step NOW.

Army and Corporate Life Differences

I am a discard of the army. Forty-five years ago, I went for the SSB interview at Allahabad. My interview went very well, but I dislocated my arm when climbing a long rope in the physical test. That was the beginning of the end of my army career. I am thrilled that my daughter and son are both Majors in the army; hence, I get to visit different parts of India where they get posted.

I joined Times of India for a while but jumped track and joined a Japanese trading house named Itochu as I thought I would savour different parts of India and the world.

I have been to twenty-four countries on business, but only the stamps on my passport prove I have been there. For instance, I would visit Dubai, Muscat, Yemen, Kuwait, Egypt, and South Africa on business and join the office on the ninth day. I have visited Japan many times but have never seen the Tokyo Tower.

In the corporate world, as a rule, people who are 35 look 45 and think like they are 55. It is the other way around in the army. The reason is that 1.3 million army folks line up for PT sharp every morning at six am.

In the army, relationships are solid. In the corporate world, relationships last only till the business lasts.

Army folks are more disciplined than corporate folks. They are rarely late for meetings, but in the corporate world, you find them rushing, huffing and puffing for meetings.

The bonding between the spouses of the army is as strong as teak, whereas it is brittle in corporate life. Politics is conspicuous by its absence in the army; however, it is abundant in corporate life.

The corporate*walas* can certainly learn a lot from the army folks. I suggest that the two should exchange roles.

If I get to live another life, I will certainly join the army.

Amreeka and Videsh—Silver Bullets?

'Do you want to go to America and settle there?' I asked my wife.

'*Subah subah mazak mat karo.* What will you do there at this age?'

'You have been a yoga teacher. We can open a yoga school there and mint money.'

'*Phir mazak.* You better try and be content here.' My dream was grounded in seconds.

My close school friend, Ron Wadhawan, who has been comfortably settled in the USA for more than 40 years, tells me that it is a land of realising your true potential, diversity and endless happy surprises. A land of possibilities, a treasure trove of vibrant cultures and infectious spirits that can make your heart dance. The spirit of innovation is in abundance in America. It knows how to party and enjoy life. It's a land of dreams, from Hollywood dreams to the dreams of striking it rich on Wall Street. It's a nation like no other—a land of milk and honey.

I believe Ron, even though I have never been to America. He is doing well because he is from an Ivy League University, has worked on Wall Street and runs a flourishing hedge fund business. But a majority of Indians who go there are not so lucky. My relatives and friends have sold their land, mortgaged their houses, done fake marriages, and are driving cars and trucks there. It is big money, but it takes a toll on your health. If a student goes there now for a good two-year course, he will have to shell out about Rs. 2 crores.

I have travelled extensively to the Middle East, Far East, Europe, and South Africa and have interacted with the Indians working in the factories there. They make money, but it is an extremely tough life. They miss their families and friends back home. They rush to India when their parents are sick or leave the world. It is a rush job because work summons.

They get dazzled by the luxury, the big cars, the good system sans corruption and the clean, healthy food. But all comes at a cost. They have to do the household chores themselves and drop the kids to school on their own as there is no support system like parents there. Unlike in India, where bribes rule the roost, they must learn to follow the law. It takes them quite some time to adjust to the new environment.

As a rule, we do not thank God for what we have but whine for what we have not got. Welcome to the whiners brigade, and quite a few Punjabis settled in Canada, the USA, and the UK fall in this category. *Unka chaudar khatam ho jata hai*—their bossy attitude is finished when they are overseas. They are used to staying around an open field in their villages and have access to errand boys there who come cheap. The village peepal tree is the rendezvous for discussing politics and backbiting. The dazzle of *vilait*, i.e., foreign shores, for these not-so-young, semi-literate Punjabi villagers who follow their kids to foreign shores is too alluring.

The cultural shock stuns them. The open space is replaced with cubby hole accommodation in flats. The children struggle to find a foothold in strange lands, doing jobs they would have looked down upon in Punjab. The politics of the village is different from overseas. The oldies try to give a village flavour by congregating in gurdwaras, which become political playfields. What seems like a Taj Mahal from afar becomes a *shamshaan bhoomi* when you are near.

In the late 80s, I was doing business with a Birla company for my Japanese employers. The Birla company wanted to open an office in Dubai and gave me an opportunity to look after it. Even though the distance was not far, the money was great and tax-free, I politely declined. I have no regrets. It was a choice.

Do you want to settle abroad and enjoy *jannat*, or are you happy in *apna* Bharat?

PART IV

Not An Accidental Rise

I just finished a riveting biography of Harsh Vardhan Shringla by Dipmala Roka in one sitting. Harsh is the Chief Coordinator of G20, ex-Ambassador of India to the USA and Thailand, and High Commissioner to Bangladesh. I have only one word—awesome.

There is nothing accidental about Harsh, lovingly called Harsha by friends. Everything is planned meticulously by him to perfection and executed to perfection. So is the book.

The six S's of Success in life, i.e., Strength, Stamina, Speed, Skill, Suppleness, and Spirit, fit Harsha perfectly. He has the seventh S, i.e., he is a Stephanian with the eighth force multiplier. He is a Sikkimese. He proves that studies and sports can not only survive, they can thrive together.

He has brought *joie de vivre* to the lives of many. A Jack Welch-type leader who produces more leaders. A team player par excellence. A *yaaran da yaar*, friends like him come once in a century.

Harsh is a product of two elite institutes, Mayo College Ajmer and St. Stephen's College Delhi, which instilled leadership and team spirit in him. His mother told me that when Harsha was young, he wanted to travel the world. Well, he is doing it by dent of his determination and persistence.

Indian Foreign Service is the perfect fit for him. He is big-hearted and has inherited humility from his family, which he wears like a badge. He is a cosmopolitan Indian and a global citizen put together. He is firmly rooted to the ground and has a soft corner for Darjeeling, where this book was launched.

Thanks to Rau's IAS Study Circle and hard work, he cleared the Civils on the first attempt and made it to the IFS. He was 15th in the merit list. France was his first foreign posting, where he met Hemal, a student, and married her. With a staff of two, he built the Consulate General of India in Ho Chi Minh City. He was back in Paris once again. The stint in the European Division in MEA followed. After that, he worked in Tel Aviv. He formed hockey teams wherever he was posted.

He was posted to the Permanent Mission of India to the UN in New York, a precursor to greater things ahead. After that, he became the Consul General of India in Durban. He continued to host Indian sports teams wherever he was posted. Stints in Nepal, Thailand, and Bangladesh followed.

He became the Ambassador of India to the USA at the young age of fifty-five. Then came the dream job of the Foreign Secretary, a job for which every IFS officer yearns. In that post, he met many business and social delegations, raising India's stature in the diplomatic world.

He is presently the Chief Coordinator of G20. India is the President of the same. This is not the end of an illustrious career. I see many more accolades and responsibilities to follow.

I recommend this book for aspiring civil servants and those in the public sector. It will help you to fully grasp India's foreign policy and the behind-the-scenes efforts these dedicated officers are making. The book should become a textbook in International Relations classes and should find a place in all libraries in India and missions abroad.

If you have not read the book, the loss is yours, my dear friends.

Nation First by Shikha Akhilesh Saxena—A must read

Shikha comes from the word *shikhar,* which means peak. Shikha's husband, Captain Akhilesh Saxena, is a decorated Kargil War hero who was badly wounded in battle. During his recovery, he spent almost a year at Base Hospital, Delhi Cantonment. Like a true soldier, he did not let adversity buckle him down and bounced back after leaving the army, which he loved, with a heavy heart.

Akhilesh topped the FMS Delhi exam and is presently Vice President at Tata Communications. He has proved that *faujis* are as intelligent as the bright kids from the bluest of blue-chip institutes—they are *hat ke.*

Shikha dreamed of penning a memoir from an army wife's perspective. She worked hard on the unseen journey of a first-time, trepidant author during the Covid period. She enjoyed the topsy-turvy journey and, with a dream start, has soared like an eagle in the writing world.

Akhilesh has soared along with her, guiding her and inspiring her. He narrated his first-hand experience of ground zero of the Kargil War in 1999 in detail and with precision, which was won by our forces from the verge of defeat. Shikha has a *hunar* of playing dexterously with words, her narrative is racy like a thriller, and the reader gets completely absorbed in it. I finished the book in one sitting. She has proved that *jannat paane ke liye kuch karna parta hai.*

Media moghul and serial entrepreneur Dr Annurag Batra, who publishes twenty-seven magazines in different fields, was one of the vociferous army supporter star panellists on stage besides Gen V.P. Malik and Air Chief Marshal B.S Dhanoa who spearheaded and led the Kargil War with aplomb along with Barkha Dutt, who covered the Kargil War when she was only Twenty-six.

Annurag, a true soldier at heart, narrated with candour how he desired to become an army officer, cleared the NDA exam but missed the bus thanks to being 1.5 kg overweight. The army's loss is the media world's gain. He exhorted youngsters to join the forces where they would learn leadership, teamwork, discipline, and bonding, which lasts for a lifetime. He spoke *dil se.*

When the Q&A session came, I was the first to raise my hand. I introduced myself as a proud *fauji* father with two kids, a daughter and a son in the army, who could not make it to the elite service because of being overweight. The audience laughed and clapped at the same time. My day was made. My question to Shikha was, *'Beta,* why did you dump an IAS officer who could have wielded more power, an Infosys and a Star Plus boy who would have earned more money and choose a dark but handsome *fauji* of medium height, Akhilesh? Also, does he take orders from you like they do in the *fauj?'* Everyone laughed again.

The graceful *dulhan* of the day replied with poise and confidence personified, 'It is a question of choice. I chose to marry an army officer. I am very happy, and I am certainly the Boss at home.'

A lot of people came up to me and complimented me. It was nothing but plain initiative on my part that helped me conquer the day. Buy the book, and you will understand why Nation should be First. You will understand the tumultuous turmoil and bravery of the men who fought a real battle, the challenges of army wives who are at home, praying and giving solace to the family members of the heroes who have become martyrs or have been injured. You will have tears in your eyes and salute them.

Well done, Shikha. More power to your pen.

Shikha can become an inspiration for other *fauji* wives as their lives are very adventurous. Different stations, different surroundings, living in and out of suitcases, living sans your husband when he gets a border posting, delaying motherhood—it is certainly not easy. They need to share their stories and struggles with the world. I requested a very bright and beautiful Mrs Sangwan, whom I accosted at the high tea after the launch, to pen her journey too. I hope she does it. Good luck to her.

Nation First by Shikha Akhilesh Saxena

'Kise mulkh yan desh di kaum andar,
Jadon vaah azaadi di vagdi e,
Aus mulkh de sachean aashikan nu,
Rehndi hoshe na sees te pag di e'

(Whenever there is a wave of a country's honour,
At that time the real heroes of the nation do not care
about their life or their turban, which is the symbol of
honour.)

I was transported back to 1999 when India won the Kargil War from the jaws of defeat. The author, Shikha, brilliantly portrays the war and a war within the war in the minds of the *sherni* wives and family members of the bravehearts fighting a real battle.

The hero, Captain Akhilesh Saxena, gets wounded badly and is hospitalised for more than a year at the age of 24 when he had been married only for a few months. He bounces back like Muhammad Ali, topped the Faculty of Management Studies Delhi batch and is now Vice President of Tata Communications. He and Shikha are cross-crossing the country, inspiring youth and making the corporate*walas* sit up with awe and think, 'If he could do it, why can't we? Why didn't we join the *fauj?*'

A riveting book indeed, which is a page-turner. It has soul and is *hat ke* from the other books on war I have perused recently, which lack depth. A web series needs to be made on this story.

If you don't read the book, the loss is yours. You will miss out on many valuable life lessons, which are more precious than the Kohinoor diamond. When you go up to Heaven or Hell *tumhari daastan tak bhi na hogi daastanon mein.*

Zindagi comes only once. Grab *Nation First* from the nearest bookstore or order online. *Aap mujhe yaad rakhenge.*

Meeting with Dominique Lapierre

On a business trip to Kolkata in 2001, I bought *Five Past Midnight In Bhopal* at the Delhi airport.

Normally, I used to stay at the Taj Bengal, but destiny had willed it otherwise, and a generous friend managed to secure a dream rate at Oberoi Grand, breakfast included. While trying to make the best of the lavish breakfast spread at the coffee shop, I was browsing through Lapierre's book when my roving eye caught sight of an unassuming foreigner in a pensive mood, munching toast.

The man's face looked similar to the writer of my book. It can't be Lapierre, I muttered to myself and hesitantly re-checked with the hostess, who confirmed that the gentleman was Dominique Lapierre indeed. He was in town for the launch of his book. The Danish pastry was given a miss with a very heavy heart as I almost hurled myself towards the famous writer. Prudence prevailed. Courtesy demanded that I should let him finish his toast at least.

Like an awed fan accosting a movie star suddenly, I fumbled for words. 'Good morning Sir. I am a great fan of yours and would be honoured to shake your hand, Sir,'

'You can sit with me.' My day was made. 'Oh, you are reading my book', the French man beamed with a 32-watt smile.

I introduced myself and requested an interview immediately, citing the reason for my business meetings during the day.

'Sorry, Rishi, but I am just leaving for an important engagement, and I am off to Delhi in the evening.' My mind did a quick mental calculation.

'Sir, I am on the same flight. Can you grant me half an hour during the air journey?'

'Sure, why not!'

'Thank you.' I beamed.

With my mind more on the exclusive interview, a coup of sorts, it was with great difficulty that I went through the grind of my business engagements. I got myself upgraded to the business class. I purchased a new camera on the way to the airport and made a mental preparation for the questions I would ask. I was in top spirits. Felt exactly like Larry King and Karan Thapar.

A student rally blocked the road; I cursed Kolkata traffic and just made it by a whisker. I looked around. Mr. Lapierre was nowhere to be seen. He could not be in the Y class. I nearly had a heart attack when the air hostess confirmed my worst fear that Mr. Lapierre had not boarded the flight.

The business-class hospitality of Jet Airways at its best just could not cheer me up. The mind was calculating the damages incurred. There was no need to share this fiasco with my family members and friends, who would have a hearty laugh at my expense. That was the only way I could get away.

Then I remembered my wife Ravi's borrowed quote after the New York 9/11 tragedy, 'We should count our blessings in celebration of being alive.' I offered a silent prayer for the WTC victims and took out my book. I smiled when I saw the autographed note on the first page:

To Rishi – with warmest good wishes always. Dominique Lapierre-15/09/2001. God had been kind.

Samsara

Lai hayaat aaye, kazaa le chali chale
Na apni khushi se aaye na apni khushi se chale!

Readers flocked around him like bees flock around honey. A young, handsome, tall, sexy boy who oozed humility and confidence signed each copy with the love a mother gives her child.

Venue—the Penguin stall at the World Book Fair. The boy seemed to have the Pathan-like status of Shah Rukh Khan in the literary world. How? I was zapped. He was too young.

I picked up Samsara from the shelf and muscled through the crowd citing my senior citizen status.

'Beta, I am Rishi, and I am 65 years young at heart. I have three published books under my belt. I have got *khushi* unlimited from them but no money. I am penning my fourth book, *Battle of the Bulge.*

'The title is very catchy. It will be a success, Uncle.'

'Wow,' I said loudly, and the seemingly sophisticated book lovers around were astonished at the loud booming voice of the fat, dark Sardar. I did not care.

'*Beta,* please write what you have said, and I will read it every day before starting to write. And last question, how long did it take to write this first book of yours?'

'Ten years, Uncle. I started writing this book when I was 17.' I was stunned.

'Then you are like Dan Brown, who writes ten pages and puts them in the dustbin before giving the final shape to one page.'

He did not say anything. He just smiled. Just like an Indian Foreign Service officer. Such maturity at such a young age. Amazing!

I have started reading *Samsara* with a lot of interest. Each page has depth and has been written with a lot of care. He is undoubtedly a genius. He has an abundance of talent. Is he God-gifted? No, it is sheer hard work.

'Haaton ki lakiron se zindagi nahi banti,
Azam hamaara bhi hissa hai apni zindagi banane ka.'

Saksham Garg is doing it with sheer hard work. The Neeraj Chopra way. If he can do it, so can you. What is stopping you? Do not wait, or as tomorrow never comes. You have to grab today like a *mehbooba* and make the most of it. Godspeed!

PART V

Ishqbaazi!

'Fitoor hota hai har umr main juda,
Khilone, mashooka, rutba aur khuda.'

Everything takes a back seat when *ishqbaazi* is involved. They become zilch. Trash. Not worth the trouble to be bothered about.

While taking a leisurely walk in the park, my roving eyes saw a young boy and girl talking sweet nothings with each other oblivious to the world around them while exercising in the open gym facing each other. Fitness was the last thing on their mind—love was. They seemed to be planning their Garden of Eden.

The girl was the daughter of a conservative friend who would have had a heart attack if he were to know his daughter was doing *ishqbaazi* in the park.

An ambitious child who desired to achieve something in life. I had deliberately decided to talk to her in English only when she came to our house, as it was not her forte. I discussed current affairs with her as she wanted to sit for the civil services exam. I did not disturb her while she was taking a round of the park.

When she came to our house, I complimented her, 'Very good, *beta.* You are exercising and walking. You should continue and focus on your studies too. The next three or four years can make or break your life.'

'Sure, Uncle. Thank you for inspiring me. ' I hope she understands the hidden meaning of my words.

Nothing has changed. *Ishqbaazi* was also in vogue fifty years ago when I was in school. A charming, beautiful girl studying with us was the cynosure of all eyes. There were more than ten desperate *majnus* trying to woo her, but her eyes were on an intelligent guy who shared the bond of music with her. Their love was hidden from all. I happened to see their love story by chance when our class took a two-day trip to the school farm in Chhatarpur, Haryana.

On a dark night, when the moon took a back seat for them only, they left the group and trudged to a lonely narrow path. I was following them not as a spy but by sleight of hand and had the privilege of enjoying their love songs in low voices for each other. They are married to different people now, unfortunately, and are trying to cement love on a new turf.

At the 25th reunion of our school, quite a few of us got together. The one-time hot and most sought-after girl also came. Like Cleopatra, she had maintained herself well. Age had not withered her, but she was a little faded and plump, and the little dark circles below her eyes told a different story if noticed carefully. But she stood out even though she was not Zeenat Aman, the favourite heroine then.

The boys, oops, middle-aged men with protruding bellies, drooled over her. They forgot their wives. They forgot the dainty dishes for which they had paid a princely sum and raced towards the prize like Usain Bolt would towards the finishing line. Everyone wanted to be the first one to meet her, impress her. She still had that aura. Men will remain men. Lovers at heart pining for their unconquered love even after marriage.

Ishq has been in existence for thousands of years. It was supreme and will remain supreme. Heer-Ranjha, Laila-Majnu, Romeo and Juliet have proved it. Bulleh Shah and Shakespeare are being quoted and read even today for their *gyaan* on love. A 33-year-girl singer, Taylor Swift, has taken the music world by storm like the Beatles did in the 60s. Her lyrics on love and heartbreak have compelled universities like Stanford and New York to start courses on her music. *Wah! Kya baat hai.* Such is the power of *ishq.*

My take, and I am talking from experience, as I have had a royal dump in *ishq*p. When you are young, focus only on your studies and career. You will get a good girl if you are well well-placed in life. You will be the most suitable boy. Salman Khan can get a beautiful, young, intelligent girl even at fifty-five. So can you. You are still young. *Ishqbaazi* can wait. The choice is yours. *Muaff karna.*

Amorous Men—baaj nahin aate!

'It takes twenty years for a woman to make a man of her son,
And another twenty minutes to make a fool of him.'

Why are there so many Brij Bhushans in India? Why do they have filthy mindsets? I am sure their parents did not instil such filthy values in them. They must have sisters and *bhabhis* at home.

When I was in college about 44 years ago, our athletics team used to be sent to Lawrence School. Sanawar every year to practice. I vividly remember the train journey where the boys were at their boisterous best. A very beautiful lady was lying on the berth across our seats. She had one toe missing on her left leg. The roving eyes of the boys were fixed on her in the same way they would be engrossed in books during an exam.

We were diffident *darpoks* then and did not dare to start a conversation with her. She was wide awake and was looking at us with inquisitive eyes. They were mischievous. They seemed to say something. But the opportunity was wasted, and the team discussed her face, eyes, and clothes even after we had reached our destination. Just like serious students would discuss the ethics or the history paper while preparing for the Civil Services exams. Such is human nature. *Dil to paagal hai! Bhatak jaata hai.*

A beautiful friend of mine who has maintained her weight, grace, aura, and charisma even after crossing the sixty-year mark had some work from a senior IAS officer. He was prompt in doing this favour but started calling and messaging her to join him for a cup of coffee. She told him she was busy with professional commitments, but he wouldn't stop. Like a dedicated stalker, he made her life quite difficult.

The lady discussed her peculiar problem with her husband, who is a wise man. He suggested she meet the eager oldie along with him. When she informed the bureaucrat, he made it very clear that he wanted to go out alone with her. She was forced to block him. Such are men. Even the ones who hold responsible public dealing positions. They need to visit a psychiatrist. Or their wives should take them there.

Deciphering Women!

It can become an extremely intricate puzzle. You can never know what's in their heart and mind. The brightest minds have failed. I believe even the Gods must have been confused and gone crazy. Is there a formula for understanding women? I believe there is no magic wand. How does one handle a woman and make her happy? Professors at Harvard can teach you leadership skills, business and time management, happiness, health, and whatnot. But they cannot teach you this art. Even Chat GPT and Threads will fail.

When a young woman is decked up, you can make out that a man is involved. Mid-aged women choose the flashiest clothes when they go to kitty parties. It's a to-see and to be seen culture. Older women wear the best dresses when they go to functions and hunting sprees to find suitable matches for their kids. All three categories put their best foot forward. Best manners and attitude go hand in hand.

When you woo a woman, there is always a conflict in your mind which is more nerve-wracking than an IIT entrance exam or sitting for the Civil Services. Will I succeed?

The triumphs and disasters of your thoughts are like scaling Mt Everest and falling into the unknown pits of hell. The mind is tormented like the mind of Hamlet in Shakespeare's drama. The drama kills you slowly, softly like liquor. You forget everything: your family, your work, your exercise, your meditation. Your sleep goes for a six like a cricket shot goes out of the stadium.

Men get smitten easily, get duped easily, will move wherever the girl wants, and get twisted, turned, and tortured easily. It is rarely the other way around.

Women can think and juggle a million things at the same time. They are practical and can keep secrets, unlike men, who can be seen through very easily. They have high taste in everything—dresses, shoes, food, boyfriends, and husbands. Their tactics are as good as a commando.

I used to work in a company many years ago, and there was a girl who was neither beautiful nor intelligent nor highly placed but had a trump card. The brand of the organisation was an automatic good sign, and she was very ambitious. She made it clear during the lunch-hour small talk that she would accept a well-placed match, handsome, rich, had his own house and, most importantly, sans parents-in-law troubling her. The wonder of wonders, she got one.

There was another sharp, intelligent girl I knew during college time. She had a steady boyfriend who was brighter. They were both preparing for the IAS exam and told everyone around that they would marry. The girl made it. The boy didn't. She dropped him like a rotten orange and married a guy training with her at the academy in

Shimla. She retired as an Additional Secretary, and so did her husband. The boy was forgotten and consigned to the dustbin of history. No one knows what he is up to.

I salute this unique tribe and sometimes wish I had been a woman. The sleight of hand could have played better. Wishful thinking indeed! I will have to wait for the next life if there is one.

If my readers have an alchemist formula, please do share. It could be helpful for others. You will be doing a great *punya*.

Tu Jhoothi, Main Makkaar—
Not Ms Zindgi

A must-see flick for want-to-be fitness freaks and people looking for exotic honeymoon locations. Sheer entertainment and great acting, histrionics, and deep kissing by the protagonists, Shraddha Kapoor and Ranbir Kapoor. Talented actors of legendary iconic actors.

Shraddha looked like the Indian Cleopatra who would launch a thousand ships and break a million hearts when she married, and Ranbir, sans any belly, looked like Adonis cum Hercules combined. I looked at my protruding belly in the dark movie hall, cursed the *pinnis, gulab jamuns* and *paronthas* that went into my tummy and vowed that I would become like Ranbir one day. Soon.

Money and time are well invested in learning about *duniya, duniya daari,* love and torture of the heart, *jhoot* and *makkaari,* family values, love, and the great advantages of Indian joint families. It was the perfect, ideal real-life culminating on the screen. I felt I was reading an awesome book.

The story moved like a trapeze artist. I am pleased that our whole family enjoyed, relished, and chewed this entertainment, whose best practices can be replicated in real life. Do go out with your family, friends, beloveds and would-be marriage partners.

Life is like an unpredictable mistress. It changes gears faster than a whore changes customers. That is why I tell my friends, *'Lutf le lo zindagi ka.'* You have only one life to live, so make the most of it because *kal ho na ho.*

Value *zindagi* and treat it like your beloved's heart, otherwise it will prove to be *jhooti* and *makkaar,* and *shaheen ho jaaye gi,* i.e., fly away like a bird from your hands *aur tum haath malte reh jaaoge.*

Aap Itne Sundar Kyon Ho?

I pose this rhetorical question to girls and boys aged 20 to 50. It catches them off guard because they don't even know me. They are surprised because some of them are dark in complexion. They are embarrassed; they blush but smile back. My next statement is, 'Ask your parents or your wife.'

I do it while travelling in metros, e-rickshaws, in parks, book launches, etc. Of course, I ensure that my safety net, i.e., my wife is with me when I shower the compliment on girls. I do not want to risk turban toppling and *hungama*. I am a peaceful man and desire to spread happiness all around. I am sure I am succeeding in my mission.

Cleopatra was dark but beautiful. So was Othello, but he married the fairest Desdemona. Michelle Obama is dark in complexion, but she radiates beauty by igniting a spark in the lives of millions of people. Quite a few people have a complex of their *dhopra,* i.e., face. This includes women and men. Why?

The eternal beauty, Laila, was dark, but Majnu was mad about her—no wonder the immortal lines of her ethereal *husn* remain intact after many centuries.

'Kise ne Majnu nu aakhya ke teri Laila kaali e,
Tan one agon hus ke jawaab ditta, teri akh nahion dekhan
wali e.
Dekh chitte varq Quran de tan onhan te sihai kaali e,
Ghulam Rasoola, jithe lar gaiyan akhiyan, te kee gori te
kee kaali e.'

(Somebody told Majnu that your beloved Laila is dark. Majnu laughed and replied that your eyes are seeing wrong. The pages of the Holy Quran are white, but the words are black. When you are in love with someone, it does not matter whether the person is dark or fair.)

My complexion is dark, but my wife finds me beautiful and handsome, and she is not joking. A warm, genuine smile can make you really beautiful. It is free of cost. Adopt it. You can carve and chisel your own beauty. You don't need any makeup.

'Never hide what makes you—You.' I am not saying it. Indira Nooyi, the ex-Pepsi top boss, said it. Become *ati sundar* by your attitude, smile, walk, and sweet talk. Your happiness will soar to the sky like an eagle.

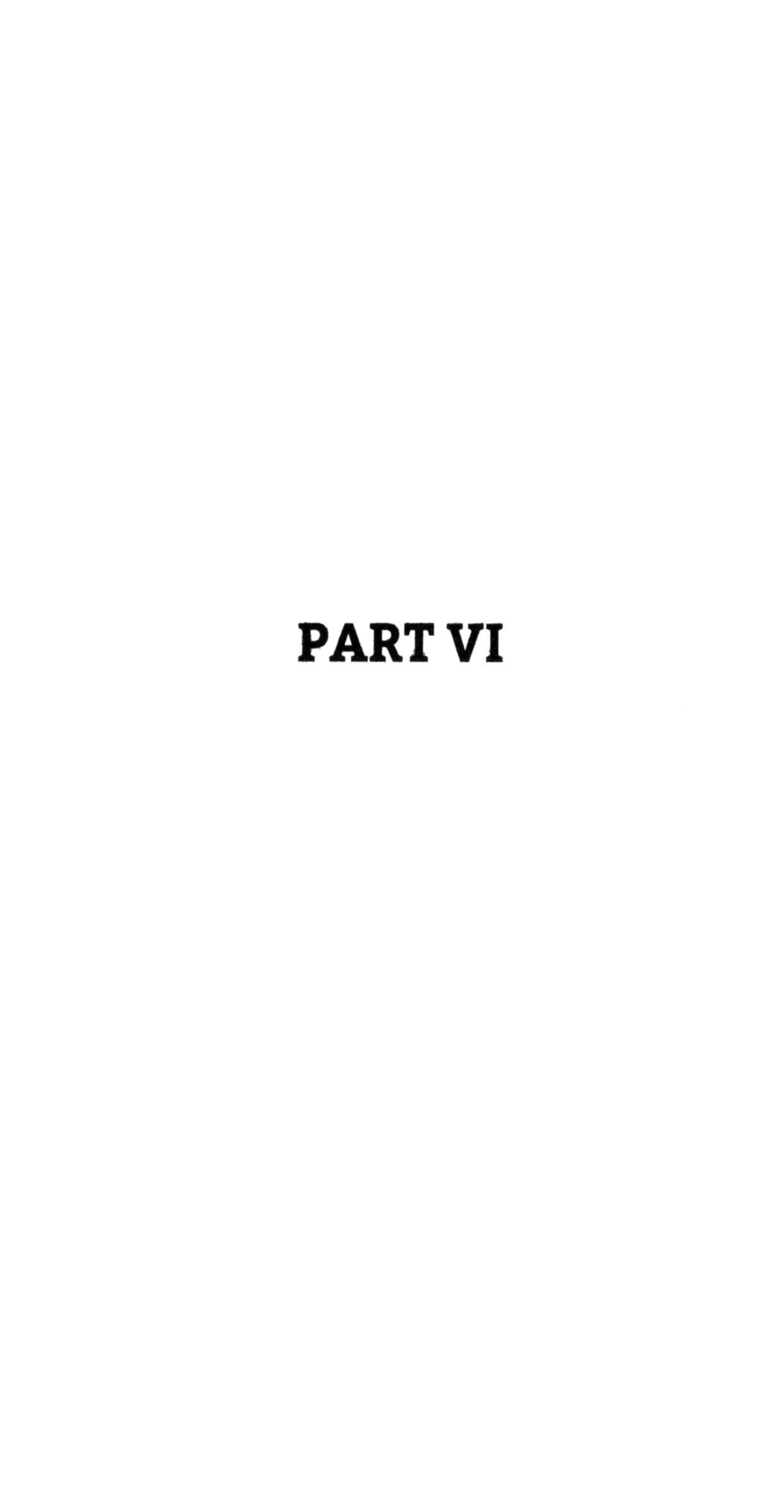

PART VI

The Taree of the IAS

The UPSC results are out, and I am very happy that girls have bagged the top four positions. They have proved that they are smarter, more hard-working, more goal-oriented and have more *junoon* than the guys. TV crews are following Ishita Kishore, Garima Lohia, and Uma Hasrath like bees follow honey. They are the flavour of the month, the poster girls and the metaphorical *dulhans* of India.

The confidence, ease, and grace they are showing is amazing. They have arrived! They will become the real *ranis* of their districts after a short while, command respect and awe, and wield tremendous power. They will become hot property. Potential suitors will woo them as they know that *zindagi haseen ho jaae gi. Bare ghar, laal batti ki gaarian,* and helpers in plenty are some of the few perks.

I was extremely fortunate to have a few close friends who made it to the IFS, IAS, IPS and Allied services. I've been invited to their get-togethers and have stayed at the official residences of a few. I found them humble, helpful, sharp, efficient and decisive. They had the *hunar* of having a helicopter view of things and the ability to handle matters and people dexterously. They were *hatke.*

I am a discard of the Civil Services fraternity. After college, I joined the Vajiram & Rao Academy, which has become Vajiram & Ravi now and is run by the son-in-law of Mr Vajiram. He is doing an excellent job. The teachers there were good, but the student, i.e., I was just not willing to put in the effort. I managed to clear the prelims but failed in the mains twice. I lost heart after that.

My parents often told me, *'Jannat paane ke liye kuch khona nahin, karna parta hai.'* I did not take them seriously. I wasted time, and time wasted me. If only I had listened to them, I too could have enjoyed the *taree* and *rutba* bureaucrats do.

The 933 candidates who have cracked the code should become inspiration engines for those who want to make it next year. But you have got to pay the price for everything in life, Bachofen's success.

Good luck, and God bless!

Hindu-St. Stephen's Rivalry!

The rivalry between the two Colleges of Delhi University has been going on for a century. Both are good and have produced excellent principals, teachers and alumni. Both have had star sportspersons, and the rivalry between them is like the one between Oxford and Cambridge universities.

I have studied in one and have been a chief guest at the other. I found both across-the-road institutions quite good, but frankly feel that their hype is more. Students with 99 percent plus marks enter these colleges are already excellent but get too much *hava* and pay the price. Fifty percent pass out, with a drop of 30 to 40 percent.

Outer campus colleges like ARSD, Ram Lal Anand, LSR, and JMC are, in some respects, better because the students there waste less time on frivolous activities. They tend to do better in the game of life. This is because the teachers there take more pains, and the students have more killer instincts and *josh*.

Jamia Millia Islamia University, which is in Delhi, is doing equally well. It is tough to get admission there now. The courses there are most sought after. The IAS Academy there has produced many winners.

My take—do not go by the name. Choose the college for the subject you like and put in the best because these are the most critical years of your life. They can make or break you.

Do not fiddle with life; otherwise, it will take you for a long ride towards Hell on Earth.

What is your opinion?

Why is St. Stephen's Going down, down, down?

Every hero becomes a bore at last. So is the case with colleges. According to the National Institutional Ranking Framework, which released the rankings, Stephen's has slid to the 14th position. Miranda has maintained its position as the top college in the country for the 7th year in a row—commendable. My daughter, a Stephanian, taught at Miranda for a while a few years ago and found it remarkable in all ways.

I am glad that ARSD and Kirori Mal are ahead of LSR and SRCC. I am sure it is thanks to the dynamic principals and the dedicated staff. Stephen's was the Usain Bolt of Education and Sports when I studied there 45 years ago. Dr W.S. Rajpal was the principal then. He took classes and played tennis with the students while sincerely performing his administrative duties. Rhode scholar math professor Ranjit Bhatia was President of Games. He used to conduct a weekly Wednesday cross-country run for all sports teams. The college ruled supreme in the sports arena.

It was deja vu during the time of Dr Valsan Thampu when two of my kids studied at St. Stephen's. Dr Thampu played tennis with the kids, ran with them up the ridge every morning, and his office and residence doors were always open. He took St. Stephen's College to the No. 1 position. He was fearless and never offered excuses. He did everything with flair and *josh*. I got an invite from him many times for interesting talks and functions.

The present principal has made it Fort Knox. A few years back, I went there at the behest of a close college friend who was out of station for important work. It was for the good of the college. I was stopped at the gate by the stern-looking but timid guards who told me rudely that the principal would only meet me if I had a prior appointment. I was disappointed and surprised.

I was fortunate to accost a senior college lecturer who met me warmly as he knew me. However, when I requested him to take me to the principal, he politely refused, citing a hilarious practice that even the teaching staff had to make a prior appointment to meet the boss. I was stunned. He refused even to share the principal's cell number. It seemed *deshat* akin to the army rule in Pakistan.

No wonder the college is sliding. When you stay in a palatial colonial house with huge manicured lawns and plenty of helpers, you start assuming *ki aap baadshah ban gaye*. You forget that you will retire one day and must adjust to a not-so-big and grand house. It will be tough going.

The principal of St. Stephen's needs to take moral responsibility and resign so that the governing body of the once No. 1 College in India gives the reins to a capable man—Godspeed.

Jashn-e-Sahir—by Alumni of SCD Government College Ludhiana

The campus was huge and spotlessly clean, like Singapore. The only college I have visited many times and found bigger and more regal is Khalsa College Amritsar.

My wife and I were received like VIPs by two young, tall, elegant, stunning girls who escorted us to the Sahir Ludhianvi Auditorium.

'Do you study in this great college?'

'No, Uncle. We teach here.' And they beamed with pride. 'And we also studied here.'

I staggered. I thought I would have a heart attack. 'Why didn't I become a teacher, and why didn't I study here?' I would have remained young forever.

'I am Vaneeta. And I am Shilpa.'

'Ohh. Then Shilpa Shetty got her name from you!' She kept quiet but smiled at my ignorance like a diplomat because Shilpa would be much older than this intelligent child.

The confident principal, Dr Tanvir, who seemed like an ex-model, rattled off the names of the illustrious alumni with pride—Sahir Ludhianvi, Dr S.C. Dhawan, NM.Vohra, K.PS Gill, Joginder Singh, Yashpal Sharma and a host of others. I thought the list would never end.

The principal invited the chief guest, Dr Amar Pal Singh, Director of Higher Education Punjab and the oldest young-at-heart alumnus, Shamsher Singh Sohi, from the 1947-49 batch, to light the lamp. He had come all the way from the USA, especially for this function. He walked up to the stage energetically, straight with pride and tears of joy in his eyes. I could see them because I happened to be sitting just behind him. Would I be able to do the same, walk the same when I went to my alma mater someday after many years? Surely.

Eleven famous alumni *shayars* of the college gave a fitting tribute to Sahir by rendering his *nazams.* They brought the house down.

The dinner organised by the college was simple but yummy and delicious. I gathered that the college has about 5000 students and about 150 teachers. How do they manage? And we talk of pressure in the corporate world. I salute the teachers and bright students of SCD Government College for their commendable role. They act as inspiration engines for other educational institutes to emulate their best practices.

A smart, young, beautiful lady who would be about forty-two came to me and asked politely, 'How was the food and the function?'

'Fantastic and out of the world. Did you study here?'

'Unfortunately, no. I teach here. I am the Head of the Economics department.'

'Wow. Where did you study?'

'I am an alumnus of Hindu College, Delhi. Have you heard of it?'

'Yeah, it is a very famous college in India. I had the privilege of being the chief guest at their cross-country race,' I responded.

A delightful and memorable evening. I met young, intelligent scholars whose energy inspired me.

I end with the famous lines of Sahir Ludhianvi.

'Na tu Hindu banega, na Musalmaan banega
Insaan ki aulad hai, insaan banega.'

May we all follow these lines.

Modern School, Delhi—
Why Is It the Best?

I am not a Modernite. However, I found it the best school among the 25-odd schools I have visited in India.

Thanks to my friend, Naresh Sachdeva, I was sitting across the table in front of Lata Vaidyanathan, the dynamic principal of Modern Barakhamba Road.

'Why do you want to shift your son from Springdales, a very good school, to our school?'

'You have the best swimming pool in Delhi, and Springdales does not have a pool. My son can practice here after his classes, and you have a competent sports department. Modern shapes the all-round personality of its students. I find them more confident than the kids of other schools.'

The lady smiled. She was a veteran in receiving compliments, especially from parents who wanted to get their kids admitted there.

'Besides Mr Naresh, can you give me three references?'

'Sure. My first reference is my Guru Rajni Kumar, who will wrangle my neck when she finds out I am shifting my son, who shares his birthday with her.'

'Great lady who commands a lot of respect in academic circles.'

'My second reference is Dr Anil Wilson, Principal of St. Stephen's College.'

'And who is your third reference?'

'My third reference is more powerful than the first two references.'

A lady sitting quietly on the sofa nearby sprang to her feet. 'I am Ketaki Sood, the Chairperson of this school, and I am quite curious to know your third reference.' She came and sat beside me.

'Please ask ten of your top swimmers from the sixth to the twelfth class who Rishi Uncle is, and if they refuse to acknowledge me, you need not give admission to my son. I have been a de facto Brand Ambassador of Modern for many years, not only in Delhi but also in other states I visit with my kids. I seize the initiative to take the mike wherever I go and do a good job.'

Admission to my son was granted immediately. He went on to Captain the Modern Water Polo team and brought laurels for the school in swimming. It was deja vu at St. Stephen's, Delhi Varsity and during Indian Military Academy training. He is a Major now and remembers Modern fondly, which gave him wings to fly in the swimming pool and life afterwards. *Modern Zindabaad!*

School ki Romance Kahaniyan!

Love is in the air in every school. It is a worldwide phenomenon. No one can shut their eyes to it. *Yeh kamaal ki cheez hai.* The lucky ones can reach Mt Everest after a herculean effort. The unlucky ones sulk and say, *'Angoor khatte hain.'* They remind me of the lines of the greatest master of love lyrics in this century, who is ruling the roost like Bulleh Shah did in the 17th century. Ron Wadhawan says,

'Ishq mein angoor khatte hote hain,
Dil ki gehraion mein udte hain chahte hain,
Jaise phoolon ko chamke chandini ki roshni,
Dard se bhar jaate hain armaan pyar ke kishti main.'

I have been to several schools in Delhi and interacted with students about this most interesting field. It is more in discussion than dull subjects like biology and mathematics. A very prestigious school in Lutyens' Delhi had a couple still talked about after many years. Jealous students would see them after school hours in the corridor holding hands. The girl often stood against a wall with the boy surrounding her with passionate arms. The girl was gorgeous and the boy handsome. The Laila-Majnu of the school fifty years ago could give lessons to Shah Rukh Khan and Kajol in the Art of Love. They are happily married.

Two teachers of a West Delhi school, which emphasised extracurricular activities more than studies and sports, were the cynosure of all prying eyes. They used to teach English and History, and I am sure they replicated the best love practices of Shakespeare and Heer-Ranjha in their amorous exercises, dodging James Bond eyes with dextrous moves. I am so glad they are happily married now.

The same school had another couple caught by the *chaprasi* kissing each other in the Prefect's room. They were taken to the office of the principal, who herself had fallen in love when she was a student in London. She did not reprimand or suspend them but told them to be more discreet in the future. The seventeen-year-olds are seventy-one now and are living a blissful life in Bengaluru.

Rab sab pe meharbaan nahi hota. A romantic couple who had a torrid affair in a South Delhi school were brazen about their love. It fizzled out after the boy went to the USA for higher studies while the girl is trying to make the best of a not-so-best bargain in Delhi. It must be torture unlimited. *Yahi Bhagwan ki leela hai.* I wonder why bad things happen to good people quite a few times. Life is certainly unfair.

The stories of fulfilled and unfulfilled forbidden love during school will continue ever onwards. Old flames die hard. *Woh dil mein rehti hain.* The unresolved crushes manifest themselves at school reunions *aur bechare pite hue aashiks* assume they are Amitabh Bachchan and the girls become Rekha for a short time, the setting of the film *Silsila* is fresh as lilies in their minds.

'Main aur meri tanhai aksar yeh baatein karte hain,
Tum hoti to kaisa hota,
Tum yeh kehti aur main aisa kehta,
Yeh kahan aa gaye hum yunhi saath saath chalte,
Teri baahon mein hai jaanam,
Mere jism jaan pighalte.'
Unke chehre pe jhoothi muskan hoti hai aur dil mein udaasi hoti hai. Tragic indeed.

Love is just a click away. It happens. It clicks sometimes and goes bust at others. Sometimes you get the prize. Other times *aap haath malte reh jaate ho aur sochte ho, kyon hua? Kab hua? Kaise hua. Yahi duniya hai. Jeena to pare ga hi. Khush reh ke jio. Muskurao.*

Beating Age

Everyone is obsessed with looking young and feeling young and takes measures to overcome age. I will tell you the *nuska,* i.e., method.

I must thank our ever-young friend, Honey, for taking my wife and me for an Urdu *mushaira* at IIC. I noticed that out of the 500-odd guests there, 80 percent were under the age of thirty. I talked to quite a few of them, and they told me that such events were good stress busters and made them interact with interesting folks different from their profession.

For instance, I was sitting alongside a young, beautiful, vivacious girl Prerna and an equally young, tall and handsome boy, Arun. It is my habit to invest more time with youngsters, and I did precisely that. They have more to offer you, are vibrant, have big dreams and are always in top spirits. They are unlike the older lot, who have personal and professional problems and are, as a rule, morose.

Prerna was from Bihar, had studied in the prestigious IIM Ahmedabad, and worked with the Government of

India body, Skill India. She shared with me the military-like disciplined life at IIM and how the classroom gates were shut even if you were a minute late. One had to work not hard but extremely hard to cope with the pressure cooker pressure there, but the fruits of this labour did come sooner than later.

Arun was working in an OTT setup and was engaged in conceptualising and preparing scripts. The three boys sitting behind me were from AIIMS. I asked them how much time they gave to studies, and they told me, 'Only about 10 in addition to their normal classes.' Honey told them that her husband had proposed to her in the AIIMS library.

Jannat paane ke liye kuch khona parta hai. You have got to pay the price for everything in life, even success. Are you willing to pay that price?

Move with people who are younger than you, smarter than you, more intelligent than you, and wiser than you. Some of their goodness will rub off on you.

PART VII

Singhs Will Be Singhs—Part 1

Ludhiana. The city of big industrialists. Munjals, Mittals, Thapars and Punjab Agricultural University. Is it the *mitti* of Ludhiana?

I greet the security entourage of the chief guest at the function. *'Sat Sri Akal!'* They reciprocate warmly while enjoying the food on their plates. They were having a quick early dinner as the boss would take time.

'You have a tough job indeed!'

'Yes, but we chose it ourselves,' a tall, dark and thin Khalsa responds.

'How do you remain so fit?' I asked just as a student asks his teacher about the country's economy.

'Ten cups of tea a day and 3-4 pegs of whisky every night is the trick.'

'Ohh, but I don't drink,' I responded with a sullen face.

'Then start this best practice immediately, and you will become thin,' they responded in chorus and had a hearty laugh at my expense.

'To be or not to be,' I say to myself. Should I start drinking now if I have to win the Battle of the Bulge? I think I should.

The smart Singh stood out because of his imposing well-tied turban. My poor crumpled turban, which I had tied with great care, paled in comparison to his. I started having an inferiority complex. 'Why, why, why?'

Singhs Will be Singhs—Part 2

The Bengaluru-Delhi flight was jam-packed. The moment the seat belt sign was switched off, the fat Khalsa, with his tummy protruding out like a pregnant woman, brandished a medium-sized whisky bottle from his coat pocket. He hid the whisky bottle like a priceless treasure in his pocket, before asking the air hostess for two glasses and water.

The moment the glasses came, he made two large pegs, put very little water and offered one glass to me.

He was shocked when I told him I was a teetotaller.

'Singh ho ke daru nahi peende! E kidan ho sakda e?' With a heavy heart, he gulped down the pegs in a jiffy. He finished the bottle quickly and immediately went off to sleep. He did not wake up for dinner.

Just as the flight was landing, I nudged him to wake up. He woke up startled. The air hostess announced, 'Captain Vikram Singh and the crew thank all of you for flying Vistara. We hope that you have had a pleasant flight. We share the good news that we have landed twenty-two minutes before time.' The passengers clapped.

The Singh *saab* sitting next to me was wide awake and roared with pride and glee in his eyes, 'After all, Singh *hai na* but *saala* pilot *bari* rash driving *kar rayaa hona.*' There was laughter all around.

Devious Dogs and Petrified Morning Walkers

The scene is akin to the movie *Darr,* a blockbuster about two decades ago. Like Shah Rukh Khan in the film, about 20 species of the canine variety put the fear of God in the minds of the morning walkers at Rajouri Garden near my residence. Like Juhi Chawla in the movie, girls from 20 to 60 are nervous. Unlike Sunny Deol, the young-at-heart *booras* and the boys forget their commando instincts, clutch their *dandas* or *dandis,* and move as if they are in enemy territory in a covert operation.

The dogs of all shapes and sizes, black and white, brown too, are fresh in the morning and hungry. They seem geared up for the ambush. The assault comes without any warning. It can come from behind, the side, or the front. The victim is caught unaware. They bite your leg, tear your track pant or *salwar,* and run away before you react.

The victim cringes and curses about coming to the park and scampers back home to get a tetanus injection with a pained, disgusted look. The other walkers, who have stopped in their tracks like statues, start discussing the menace. Everything else is forgotten—politics, bad bosses, kids, and friends. It is a daily affair. The *Darr* syndrome begins once again the following day.

Animal lover Maneka Gandhi's bill favours the canines. Dog lovers love it, and others hate it. It is like the tug of war in the state of Delhi between AAP and BJP. People who know the law state that you can be hauled up if you hit a dog. If by any chance the dog is killed and you are caught, the penalty is very stringent.

The MCD vans come once in a blue moon. The dogs seem to have informers in the MCD offices. The moment the extremely fat and struggling guys come with their nets, the dogs take off in a *jhund* barking a loud warning to their friends and speed away like Usain Bolt or PT Usha. This is India. The confidence of the dogs is contagious. The fear of the walkers is justified. Nothing has changed for the last 45 years. I have been frequenting the park on and off. It is an all-India affair.

In the last three decades, I have travelled to twenty-five countries. Only once in Paris did I see a docile stray dog walking gently like a lamb on the busy street. He seemed well-behaved. Others were tied to their leash by their owners. Friends, do you have a solution? Pray enlighten us.

Rehris, Rishwat, Police, and MCD
(Municipal Corporation of Delhi)

Every morning, after finishing my snail-paced walk, I accost a few *fruitwalas* outside the park on the way home. I buy fruit ordered by my wife and start conversations with them. They have a tough life. As tough as the army or the corporate world—I say probably tougher.

My friend, Uday, has to be up before four am, seven days a week, to go to the Azadpur Mandi in Delhi in an e-rickshaw to procure quality fruit. His son, who is studying, brings the *rehri* to the accredited place from home before seven am to make his father's life a little easier.

I see well-dressed ladies, gents, and couples in expensive tracksuits with their protruding tummies haggling with Uday to reduce his price. Some threaten to buy fruit from the vendor across the road. With a heavy heart, Uday has to accept their demand for fear of losing a regular customer. He says he is usually done for the day by three pm once all the fruit has been sold. Once he returns home, he has his first meal of the day. Some days, when he is famished, he eats one banana.

Uday has to pay Rs. 500 monthly to the *thulla,* i.e., the policeman, and the same amount to the representative of MCD. Why? To park his *rehri.* At least once in three-four months, the area is raided, and the MCD van confiscates the *rehris.* They have to show that they are doing a good job despite paying bribes regularly and without fail.

This rotten practice is a pan-India affair and has been prevalent for a long time. The bribe is shared proportionately from down up. There must be very few staff members who dare to say no. The corrupt staff will buy *lambi gaaris* in someone else's name, and their wives will procure *mehngi saaris* and gold. More often than not, their kids will be spoilt because they do not know the value of money. I feel sad that they will have a tough life when forced to face reality later. Like *kabooters* with closed eyes, they are oblivious to what life is about.

Uday's son is studying to become a chartered accountant. The boy is sincere, and he will surely make it. Uday, like his name, will shine in his son's success. *Ache din* will come for the family soon. When will they come for India? As a full-time optimist, I hope it will be in my lifetime. What do you think? Will India become a corruption-free country? Like Singapore or Saudi Arabia?

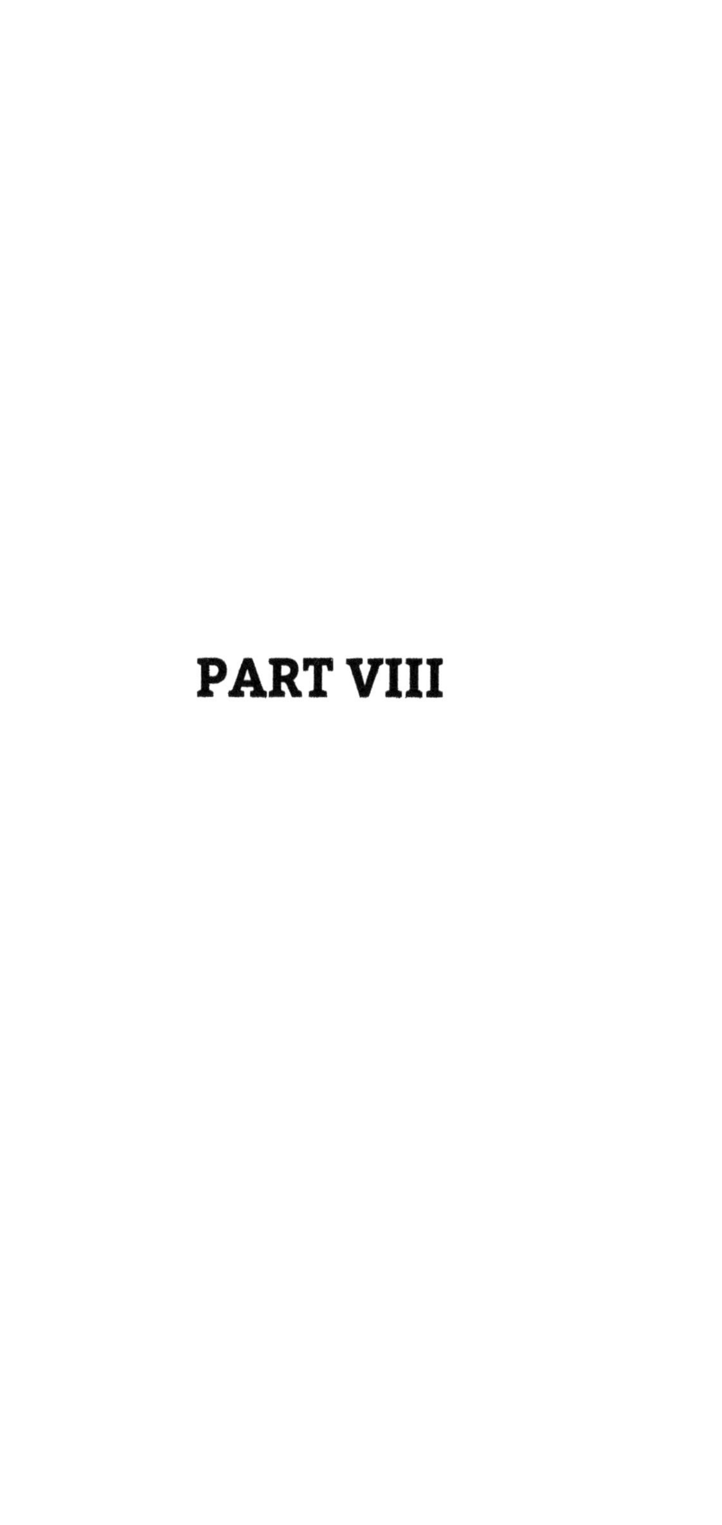

PART VIII

Holi Celebrations for All, but Work as Usual for Quite a Few

'*Happy Holi,* Munna *beta.* You need not collect the litter today. Celebrate Holi.'

'How can I do that, Uncleji? It is my duty. Moreover, I lost my young son recently.' He was devastated. I was stunned. God had been unkind to him.

I went for a walk. I wished the six guards on duty at the colony gates. They have to work 12 hours a day, 365 days a year. The day they take leave, their pay is cut. Life is indeed unkind to these sincere souls who come from different parts of India to earn money.

I went to the C.K. Birla Hospital to wish a friend who was admitted there. My mind rewound to thirty years ago when I visited NEC Corporation in Jaipur for business. NEC was a part of the CK Birla group. The President had offered me a job there. He said they were planning to open an office in Dubai, and he would be happy to induct me to the top position there. I thanked him but politely refused, as I had no intention of working outside India.

I got friendly with the staff standing outside CK Birla Hospital and admired them for their noble service. One of them staying in Ghazipur was boarding a metro at six am to reach his place of work at eight am. He was catching the 8:30 pm train and would reach his house at 10:30 pm.

Wow! Society is oblivious to these real heroes. I salute them.

Religion of Wealth!

Corporates are the fastest-growing religion in the world. Whether you want this neoreligion (wealth) or not is your choice.

A tug of war is going on between the traditional religion and the neoreligion. People are confused as they try to follow both. Corporate values and traditional values are like two opposite poles.

The new religion has three groups, i.e., winners, mediocre, and losers. Winners have to master problem-solving skills. We have a choice to become a winner. We have to follow the path and rules of the wealth of the neoreligion game. To become a winner, you have to start the process of change.

How to achieve change? Unlearning, relearning, and cognitive reshaping.

How to win the corporate game? You have to follow the five virtues of the new corporate world, i.e., sex, greed, anger, ego, and attachment, to go up the ladder.

What are the five evils of the corporate world? They are truth, compassion, contentment, humility, and love.

It is a paradoxical situation, and an individual must choose. In traditional religion, God is Almighty. In neoreligion, money is Almighty. In India, wealth is Almighty.

My take: wealth is not what you have or how much you have. It is how you use what you have. My wealth is the few friends and relatives who make life worth living. I truly feel I am a wealthy man compared to a millionaire or a billionaire. This is because I have what he will never have—enough.

Be content, be healthy and be happy.

PART IX

My Memorable Wedding—
Started with a Bang!

All weddings are memorable. Mine was more. It was my first wedding, and I was nervous as I did not have the experience of Richard Burton and Liz Taylor. I was so anxious to rush to the wedding venue that I forgot to go to the gurdwara, which I used to do every day. I requested my mama, a colonel in the army, to reverse the car. He was hesitant because it was considered a bad omen. I insisted, and he had no choice.

Just as my uncle was turning right on the Ring Road towards Dhaula Kuan in Delhi, a truck coming at breakneck speed hit our car. It screeched to a halt more than 15 feet away. The engine was smashed, and smoke came out of it like it does in a *shamshaan bhumi.*

My poor turban, tied with the utmost care, twisted sideways as my head hit my cousin, who had come from the UK. She started giggling at my poor state of affairs. Her countenance changed immediately after she realised the gravity of the matter.

All hell broke loose. Shrieks came from the womenfolk, the choicest of abuses from the men. The driver of the truck, who was drunk, was pulled out and beaten black and blue by everyone who came in contact. My *bua,* who was illiterate, insisted that we call off the wedding.

I was sitting like a poor cock waiting to be slaughtered. No one asked for my opinion. I was dying to get married. My father, a decisive man, had the final word. 'Rishi, go back home and tie your turban again. You look like a person who has been banged before his wedding.' He wanted to bring an element of fun into the tense atmosphere. He did.

Stephen Hawking may say God does not exist, but I believe He does. Marriages are made in Heaven and can become heavenly if you put in an effort, learn to adjust, and remain a friend to your partner. Marriage is not a square or a rectangle, or a triangle. It is made of little dots. One has to join these dots to attain Nirvana on Earth.

My Disastrous Date with a Jyotish

'Where are you going alone on a cold Sunday?' My wife was anxious about my plans as she had others with me on the same day.

'I am going on a date.'

'*Sudhar jaao, ab tumhare bacche bare ho gaye hain,*' she admonished me.

'I am going on a date with a very big *jyotish.*'

'Really? I will come with you.'

'But you don't believe in *jyotishi.*'

'Even you don't, then why are you going?' My better half shot back with a twinkle in her eyes.

'I am just going for curiosity, and I don't have to pay anything as the appointment has been taken by one of my big-shot friends.'

'All the more reason for me to come along,' responded my frugal wife.

When we reached the lobby of Hotel Lalit in Connaught Place, I called the cell of the futurologist.

'*Namaskar Rishi ji, mein* coffee shop *mein hun,* corner table *pe betha hun. Aur maine safed kurta pajama dala hua hai.*'

I spotted him immediately. He was talking to a man who was a bigwig from the opposition party. After saying *namaste,* I played patience with my wife at a table nearby. My turn came quite soon. He beckoned me to join him when he was done with the politician. I introduced my wife and asked him the price he would charge.

'Aap ne kuch nahin dena. Bhai saab ka phone aa gaya tha.'

'Lekin maine akele aana tha.'

'No problem, *isse aap* free gift *samajhiye.'*

'Shukriya,' I responded with alacrity.

I requested him to start with my wife. He told her quite a few interesting things she wanted to hear, which mainly revolved around the welfare of our kids. It elevated our hearts. She did not have much to ask, and whatever he told her in the next seven minutes was enough. She was more curious about my hand.

The fat *jyotish* with piercing eyes looked at my hand like a lover looks at his beloved's while holding hers. *'Aap kya poochna chaahte hain, koi* specific *cheez?'*

'Kya main Hindustan ka Sports Minister banoonga aur kya mera parivar khush aur tandrust rahega?' I asked, point blank. His response came like a bullet that hit the hearts of both of us.

'Aap ki to shaadi inke saath honi hi nahin chahiya thi. Aur mein heran hun ki aap abhi tak ikatthe hain.'

My mouth opened wide. But my wife, who is generally reticent and hardly opens her mouth, said, *'Mein yahaan nahi beth rahi,'* and stormed out of the coffee shop.

It has been quite a few years since that day, but I am at the receiving end even now as my wife shared the incident with her family and friends and ends her story with *'Mujhe lagta hai Rishi aur voh fraud jyotish mile hue the.'*

Poor Dulhas and Dulhans!

The music is at full blast. People are enjoying the grand moment. Family members receive guests with *bateesi* out and aching backs, and friends make merry with their girlfriends or make new ones on a virgin turf. The live band or the singer makes it difficult for the people to hear what is being said. Everyone is in a *masti* mood except for the groom. He is lost, alone, nervous, and anxiously awaiting the bride. He wants the show to finish as soon as possible so that he can start sweet nothings with his wife. But this is India, where norms have to be followed.

The snack tables are jam-packed despite the waiters going around with the delicious dishes. The maximum rush is at the bar. The young, the old, girls sans a care in the world are having the time of their lives. Some friends take a drink to the groom and ask him to gulp it to gain confidence. His heart says yes, but his mind stops him. He does not want to become a laughing stock.

Guests are more interested in the dinner being served as they have to return home to go to the office the next day or send the kids to school. And they have given the *shagun.* How can they forego the food? Their tummies be damned. When the announcement that dinner is served comes, the guests rush towards the tables as if there is no tomorrow. The poor bride is forgotten. She could be delayed in getting ready or caught in a traffic jam. Chicken curry and *daal* spill on people's suits, and a verbal duel starts with choices of abuses if it is a Punjabi wedding.

The demure bride, all decked up, enters while there is commotion all around. Her close friends accompanying her are as well dressed, if not more. They are wooing potential life partners. Barring the bride's parents, who are shifty and have a million thoughts in their minds, others are in top form without a care in the world. Like established dress designers, they have their expert comments on the bride's dress, the food, the venue, and whatnot.

When the bride finally sits on the stage with her lifelong partner-to-be, the photographers and the video team take over. They make the protagonists pose better than Shah Rukh Khan and Deepika Padukone. It is fine if the boy and girl are having a love marriage; otherwise, both are at a loss for words. The girl is thinking of her second innings; 'When will she attain sync with him and his family?' 'When will she control the boy and his family?' The boy is engrossed in thoughts of adjustment with her, and she with his family in case they have to stay in a joint family.

The *var mala* time finally comes, and there is a lot of jumping up and down. This is just the rehearsal for many more jumps and falls in married life. In Hindi films, the *var mala* culminates in marriage and bliss afterwards. In real life, it is just the beginning. Marriage is a long, long journey. You have to put in effort to make it bliss. Gear up for it. Good luck!

Beeg Fight and Truce—That's Marriage!

The war between Russia and Ukraine has lasted more than fifteen months, and no truce is in sight. The reason—big egos. The same holds true for marriage too. If you are willing to compromise and accept each other's faults sportingly, the topsy-turvy journey can become a blissful ride; otherwise, it can become Hell on Earth.

I admit that I am a short fuse. My *para* immediately shoots up and drops like a thermometer in boiling water and ice. Well, I suffer for my deeds. You have got to pay the price for everything in life, even anger.

My *sarkar,* i.e., my wife, and I had an excellent South Indian meal at the restaurant Juggernaut last night. The name is a twist from the original name Jagan Nath for the benefit of the *goras* and the *angrez* Indians. The food was delicious and the ambience was quaint. We were delighted. I ate plenty and slept like a log.

Just as I was dreaming of my next wonderful article, I was woken up by the boss and ordered to get ready for a walk. After a short silent prayer, I was all set to conquer the day. We had just crossed the gurdwara on the way to the park when I said something that irked my wife. She felt it was too blunt and brazen. 'You should try to be diplomatic and always think you are talking to Harsha (a close friend who is a top-notch functionary in the diplomatic services).'

I said, 'No, I will be Sacha Singh.' My 'temper' shot up like a rocket. When my mother was alive, she often admonished me, *'Teri zubaan ne tera satyanas kar diya hai. You can conquer the world if you control your tongue.'*

'I'm returning home,' came the response. I followed her like a timid puppy. I apologised half-heartedly while giving her a mild hug on the road. 'People are watching us,' she responded immediately. She was embarrassed. Luckily, there were very few.

All is well on the home front now. *Halwa* was prepared as a reward for my *dil se maafi*. That's what my wife thought. She is simple. Just like my 46-inch tummy, be damned.

'Patio, galti karo to jaldi maafi maang lo. Nahin to... You know better.'

Marriage, especially in India, is a long, challenging *safar* with many ups and downs, like ocean waves. You and you alone can put MAGIC into it. Just Do It!

Marriages and VIP Guests

About 85 years ago, a young handsome boy who was not yet settled was getting married to the girl he adored in Modern School Delhi, where they both studied from nursery onwards. The boy was Khushwant Singh, the son of Sir Shobha Singh, one of the contractors who built the Rashtrapati Bhavan, Connaught Place, and Modern School. Khushwant went on to become a famous writer, historian, and Member of Parliament.

In one of his columns, he wrote that he and his wife were overshadowed, obliterated, and literally forgotten from the grand reception in Delhi, where the biggest bigshots converged. From Mohammad Ali Jinnah, the Founder of Pakistan later, highly placed *goras, goris,* ministers, the then Ambanis and Adanis, bureaucrats, and the who's who of India. No one looked or had time for the poor couple. This is the tragicomedy of high-profile weddings. They become venues to see and to be seen and network.

I am told that the Bollywood Badshah Shah Rukh Khan charges only Rs. 8 crores to dance at a wedding, and Katrina Kaif Rs asks for Rs. 5 crores. Then what happens to the poor bride and bridegroom? They become nonentities, and I strongly feel they should leave the wedding venue to explore each other and attain happiness and bliss. Customs, decorum, back-breaking photo sessions, and *shagun* force them to stay put with a heavy heart.

Weddings in Punjab have to be seen to be believed. The tops in their field are invited—all the fields. I attended the wedding of the son of an industrial friend in Ludhiana, Punjab. The *milni* ceremony, which is supposed to be done by the close relatives of the two parties where they put garlands around the necks of very close relatives of each side, had all the biggies as extra VVIPs. The city's Deputy Commissioner, the Police Commissioner, the SSP, and the Home and Finance Ministers of Punjab were given heavy cash packets from the girl's side along with the relatives. My guesstimate is that Rs. 100,000 was given to each person. In Punjabi *lingo,* they call it *torr,* which means 'pride'. What bloody *torr?* It put extra pressure on the girl's side.

A close friend, Avinash, and I attended the reception of another close friend, Harpreet, in Amritsar about twenty-five years ago. He was then a correspondent with the *Hindustan Times* newspaper, and his father Brig. Mohinder Singh was the Chairman of the Amritsar Improvement Trust. First, our wives, who wanted to deck up like Sharmila Tagore and Sadhana, delayed us by about two hours. We were caught in a massive traffic jam where everyone seemed to be heading towards Harpreet's wedding. The security vehicles of the VIPs made it worse. The long spiralling line of VIPs going on the stage to wish the couple Sandeep, lovingly called Typsy, and Harpreet made it a back-breaking exercise despite the waiters running around with scotch, cold drinks, *murgas, shammi kababs,* and many other dishes. No one was bothered about the couple, who were tired after standing for hours and giving big smiles, I wonder whether real or not, while bending down to touch feet, shaking hands and getting photographed.

The most memorable wedding I attended was that of Dr Anu, the daughter of my guru, Dr Valson Thampu, then the principal of St. Stephen's College Delhi, in Bhiwani, Haryana. Our entourage comprised only seventeen members. When my rickety car, in which Dr Thampu and I were travelling, reached the Circuit House, it had a sudden puncture at a very wrong time. Dr Thampu jumped out of the car like an athlete, pushing it to the side. His *samdhi,* i.e., the boy's father, rushed forward to assist him. We were received by about 500 people who were the who's who of Haryana. Anu *beta* gave a virtuoso performance on the piano. Thampu Sir gave an impassioned emotional speech that brought the house down. The simple reception that Dr Thampu gave at a church in Hauz Khas Delhi was simply a class apart. Relatives, educationists, and many well-wishers were there. I was privileged to be the only student of Dr Thampu's to be invited. He shared with me later that he spent less than Rs. 100,000 on the reception. I wish other fathers would emulate his best practices.

I had retired by the time my son got married. An eminent editor of a prominent national financial daily who used to walk with me in the park every day told me that no bigshot would come for the reception as I was no longer holding a senior position. I told him flatly that what mattered the most was that my kids remain happy after marriage, and they are. We held the reception in a mess in Delhi Cantonment, and the relatives and friends made it an enjoyable affair. Did the media moghuls, ambassadors, and industrialists who came for the wedding of the editor's daughter make his daughter more happy? I doubt it.

The most forgettable VIP wedding I attended was that of my close school friend Ranjan Wadhawan at Taj Delhi. Ranjan's father was, at that time, the Director Revenue Intelligence Government of India. Everybody who was anybody had rushed from different places to attend. I was descending the stairs in front of the stage with my wife and another close friend nicknamed General Chance when I fell flat on my face. My poor turban came off. General Chance laughed heartily and said, '*Chance ki baat hai*, Rishi.'

The sophisticated women around were aghast as most had not seen a Sardar with dishevelled hair sans a turban. Poor Ranjan, who saw the scene from the VVIP seat, was shocked. He didn't know what to do because he was the *dulha* and, therefore, extremely nervous. My wife came to my rescue in my hour of misery. She picked up my turban, and we rushed to the washroom. I did not dare to go back to the hall. We took a taxi and went home without food, which I love.

Operation Chitrol at a Marriage

Chitrol is a typical Punjabi word and means shoe beating.

Usually, one associates marriages with joy and dancing. However, I attended a unique marriage in Delhi a few years back that went in the opposite direction.

About 400 *baaratis* were invited by the girl's side and were enjoying themselves having *murgas, seekh kabab, chaat,* and the five different types of food laid out by the girl's family to make the *baratis* happy.

The groom's father was drunk and was being supported by two helpers. I do not know what came over him, but when everything was going well, he asked the bride's father for a Merc and lots of cash. The latter was shell-shocked in front of quite a few guests. Like a scene from a Hindi movie, his face fell, and he requested time to discuss it with the family members.

We were all enjoying ourselves when there was a huge *hungama.* The bride's brothers, along with their friends, started beating the *baaratis* black and blue. The plates fell from their hands, the *chaat* spilt on the suits and *saaris* of women, and quite a few turbans toppled. Shoes were lost, and suits were torn as guests ran helter-skelter for their dear lives.

I am very happy for the bride. God made her kick a rotten boy out of her life. She is extremely happy presently, married to a wonderful guy who loves her and not her money bags.

Adjustment with Wife for Happiness!

Avoid fighting or arguing with your wife. You may win the battle, but you will lose the war eventually. Never mistake her silence for weakness. It's always quiet before the storm. In the worst case, she may leave you or go to her parent's house. And you will have to go there '*muhn latka ke*' to bring her back. *Taane alag milenge.* Why waste precious energy? Use it for better things. It is just not worth the trouble.

I have witnessed divorce cases going on for years. They are messy. Both sides accuse each other, and things hidden behind closed doors come out into the open. The Indian courts are a living hell. You suffer, your family suffers, and your kids suffer the most. The biggest beneficiaries are the lawyers. Whether you win or lose, they laugh all the way to the bank.

Make your *zindagi more haseen* and *rangeen* by making adjustments with your wife. Strive to make her happy, and you will be happy. *Jhuk jaao. Akalmandi karo ge. Har kisi ko mukamil biwi nahi milti.* The same is true for wives too. They will never get an ideal husband. Never ever.

I am reminded of an episode in *Kaun Banega Crorepati* when a gushing lady contestant told Amitabh Bachchan that he often comes in her dreams. The diplomatic embarrassed Big B blushes like a bride and asks her whether her husband comes in her dreams too. The innocent but courageous wife says, '*Apna husband kisi patni ke sapnon mein nahin aata.*'

More often than not, another's wife seems more attractive, better, beautiful, and graceful than your own. When it happens, remember the truism, '*Cheez mil jaae to mitti hai, na mile to sona hai.*' And you do not know the reality. *Door ke dhol hamesha suhaane lagta hain.* Your wife is the wind beneath your wings. She makes you soar like an eagle in all walks of life. Treat her like a Kohinoor diamond. Or you may lose her like India lost the Kohinoor *aur aaj tak bechara koshish kar raha hai usko vapis laane ki*—sans success. Don't become that *bechara*.

PART X

Date with God—Visit to the Golden Temple

25th December, 2012. Ms Fog nearly spoiled my date with God at the Harmandir Sahib Amritsar (Golden Temple), the Vatican of the Sikhs.

With grit and determination, I made it bite dust thanks to the strength I got from God. With a prayer in my heart and to keep a promise I had made to myself, I started from my Delhi residence at 5:30 am in the pitch dark. The dogs were the first obstacle. They got excited seeing a dark Sardar in a black turban and a black sweater. They barked excitedly at finding one more victim like them in the biting cold. They must have woken up half the neighbourhood by barking at an ungodly hour.

I did not find it funny as I trepidly walked towards the metro station near my house. I finally made it in one piece. Reaching New Delhi station was a smooth ride. I thanked Mr. Sreedharan and the Delhi Government for giving us one of the best gifts.

My obstacle race had just started. The platform was choc-o-block, with passengers jostling for space and doing the steeple chase over people who had made the platform a sleeping place. Maybe their trains were delayed. Maybe it was the cold. I did not care. Huffing and puffing, I ran up the stairs and nearly risked a heart seizure because I was cutting it very fine, and I did not want to catch the train running. I had no illusions of being Shah Rukh Khan. It was impossible to walk on the platform where the Shatabdi was to commence its journey.

The train was nowhere in sight. I thought I had missed it. I checked with a hassled passenger, who informed me that the train was delayed by five hours. I cursed the Indian Railways and then cursed myself for not checking the departure timing before starting from home. It was the third time in three years that the Indian Railways had played spoilsport with me and forced me to cancel my Punjab trip. The previous two trips were at the year-end too. In the first instance, I could not keep my promise of taking my friend Oota San to the Golden Temple. And the second was for the attendance of the marriage of the daughter of my Ludhiana friend, Monto (Rajesh Bhambi).

But I was hell-bent on ending my year on a grateful note as God had fulfilled two wishes of mine—I had become an author, and we as a family had shifted into a reconstructed house, which was my father's desire. I had promised to offer prayers at the Golden Temple within this year, i.e. 2012. And I did. I took the delayed train, stayed overnight at Jalandhar at my mama's residence and continued my journey the following day after taking a cold shower to ensure that I did not back out. I felt pleased, satisfied and at peace with myself.

Death and Obituary Speeches

Death is the only thing that can bring you to life. No matter how many milestones you chalk out, you will never be more remembered than in death, which is what makes an obituary so important.

Obituaries are published after the mortal remains are consigned to flames, and the world jumps onto the bandwagon eulogising the departed soul. Most often than not, obituaries are unwilling figments of the living imagination. Some discreetly smirk at the deceased, while others mark their disdain for the departed soul, yet all of them compose poetic verses lavishing soulless praises in honour of the one who has blissfully moved on.

Call it a psychological trip into the deliriums of my vanity, but I dream of raising my pen to ink my own obituary to keep it honest. I do not wish for others to sing praises of me, nor do I wish to be remembered through someone else's words. I wish to praise myself and get a kick out of the sheer horror some of my acquaintances will experience.

I do not expect many to attend my *chautha*. My dearest wife and kids will certainly be there. Amongst my close friends, Avinash will cry the most. He will genuinely miss me. Despite their jam-packed schedules, Harsha, Chatto, and Dr Valsan Thampu will come. Rajiv and Praveen, my *langotia yaars* from school, will certainly be there.

Dr Thampu, Avinash and Harsha will lead the list of star speakers and will shower lavish praise on me.

My dear readers, you will be surprised that I have got the audience clapping at some obituary speeches I have given because I raise the emotional quotient of the audience. Luminaries like Sir Mark Tully have complimented me on my obituary speech once, and believe me, I was thrilled.

Friends, how will you face Ms Deesth, and what sort of obituary speeches would you like to hear sitting up in heaven?

Obituary Speeches and Clapping!

'Agah apni maut se koi bashar nahi,
Samaan sau baras ka aur pal ki khabar nahi.
Laai hayat aaye, kaza le chali chale,
Na apni khushi se aaye, na apni khushi se chale.'

'You should apply for a patent for your obituary speeches, Rishi.' My learned friend, Honey Sharma, said after I had finished my *dil se* given speech at a *chautha*, which elicited a round of applause from the mourners. Very unusual, but it has happened many times. My speeches differ from the run-of-the-mill *bhaashans* with the same plot that most of the *sangat* has heard at different places.

I make it a point to give speeches which are interesting, short, and tell things many do not know about the person who is gone. I touch the hearts of the audience and narrate the good deeds of the deceased person and the family. I emphasise the importance of the role and also that as one goes up the ladder of life, the role becomes less, but the importance of the role becomes more.

I have also noticed that if the person who is oblivious of what is happening is a big shot, there is a clamour for the stage. The poor master of ceremonies has a harrowing time. The people left out leave the venue with long faces before the function is finished. Their spouses have no choice but to follow them.

There are quite a few who come to network. To see and to be seen. Their thoughts are somewhere else while the speeches are given. Only the family members and a few close ones are actually sad. For others, it is just a *dikhava*.

Quite a few of my close friends are dying to give my obituary speech. They should give one in advance while I am alive and kicking. I can make a few changes. They will have to wait quite a while as I desire to cross the century mark. We need to praise a person when they are alive rather than after he is no more. The dead do not speak. They give a damn about what you say or think about them. Do it now; otherwise, it will be too late.

PAXT XI

Sant from Kerala

Just like Jesus Christ gave his Sermons on the mount about 2000 years ago, a saintly, young, soft-spoken, erudite English teacher replicated these best practices at St. Stephen's College, Delhi. I was his student from 1974 to 1977. It is fascinating to discover some people in life. I was fortunate to accost Dr Reverend Valson Thampu, who transformed a fat, dark, *darpok* Sardar, i.e., me, into a confident, enlightened, energetic young man ready to take on the world. He used to lend me books outside the course, which opened my horizons, transported me to different lands I had never visited, and made me befriend wonderful people. Our relationship has lasted till date. It is as strong as oak. I will say stronger. Thanks to him, I have three books under my belt.

Dr Thampu has traits similar to Mahatma Gandhi. He believed in *ahimsa.* As a teacher, he would give scintillating lectures in the morning assembly and quote examples from the Bible, explaining their relevance in the present times. He believes that strong fundamentals of truth should be our top priority, and he followed these principles. He added that building ethical infrastructure is more important than building physical infrastructure.

Satyamev Jayate is the national motto, and it was and is the motto of Dr Thampu too.

Dr Thampu has always followed the winning formula of the former world boxing champion Mohammad Ali who won a gold medal in boxing at the Rome Olympics in 1960 but threw the medal in a river because of his principles. Mohammad Ali said,

'Winners are not made in gyms,
They are made from something that comes from deep within.
A dream, a desire, a vision.
They have to have last-minute stamina,
They have to be a little faster,
They have to have the skill and the will
But the will has to be stronger than the skill.'

Dr Thampu has willpower and, like an acrobat, has bounced back from adversity plenty of times. He is a perfect combination of Mahatma Gandhi and Mohammad Ali, taking the best of both. His force multiplier is that he loves tennis, and like Raphael Nadal, he is on the court during an educational battle and believes in only victory. Nothing else. The honest way. He has a strong heart with a soft corner for the have-nots and strong legs, making him move everywhere like Novak Djokovic. For him, 72 is like the new 42, just as 36 is the new 26 for Djokovic.

Nobody expected him to become the principal of St. Stephen's. Nobody wanted him to head this institution. He proved all professional naysayers and political pundits wrong by taking on the reins in 2007. He ruled the institution till 2016. The teachers didn't want him; some class four staff instigated by the teachers didn't want him and held plenty of *dharnas* against him. They had to bite the dust and were grounded, smashed to a pulp like warriors on a losing side. However, the students loved him because he did not make his office and residence Fort Knox. He followed the open-door policy, listened to their challenges, and found ways to steer them to victory.

In 2015, he initiated a year-long Citizenship Enrichment Programme where students from other colleges could also enrol. It was a one-year weekly class programme, and the fee was Rs. 1000 only. Certificates were given to students ranging from 17-71 years. It was a fun course with a lot of real-life learning thrown in. The aim was to produce a culture of responsibility and enlightenment. It was a roaring success. I was privileged to be a student there.

Dr Thampu has penned nineteen books. I found *On a Stormy Course* the best. It is about his journey at St Stephen's as a student, a teacher, a block tutor, and a principal. Not bad for a student who studied in a Malayalam-medium school till the ninth standard and was washing buffalos under his mother's orders. He certainly acts as an inspiration engine for youngsters who can learn from him how to overcome odds and come out triumphant. My wife and I had the privilege of being hosted by him for a week in December 2018 at his quaint Trivandrum home full of books and love. It was like a visit to a temple of learning, sans any frills but plenty of thrills, with discussions starting at three am.

Dr Thampu feels that religion is showbiz. No wonder many godmen are thriving as they have mastered the art of publicity and are dancing away to their gold towers and crores of cash as they do not trust the banks. He feels that a nation is its people, which includes every citizen and not citizens of a particular religion. According to him, the present government of Modi is driving propaganda and needs to do a lot more for the people to become a superpower. This is what I think Dr Thampu said. He is a soldier saint spreading the gospel of truth and love through his preachings. May he succeed in this noble mission—my prayers for him. I sincerely hope he is not put on the cross like Jesus was.

Please subscribe to his YouTube channel, *A Temple of Thoughts*. I can assure you that it will do you a world of good and give you immense knowledge. You will be a gainer—all the way. Follow the Nike model. Just do it.

Rishte and Farishte!

'Zindagi mein kuch rishte hote hain,
Aage chal kar voh farishte ban jaate hain!'

Ranjan and I studied in Springdales School in Delhi and have been close friends for the last 55 years. After college, he settled well in the USA and has lived there for 45 years. His parents were Delhi based, and I kept a close connection with them.

Forty years ago, I got a chance to visit Japan on business. I was on cloud nine. I was to go suddenly, and I did not have a passport. My boss yelled at me, and I became the butt of jokes of my colleagues. Being a child of teachers, I never thought I would ever go abroad. Now that God had given me the opportunity, it was slipping away like sand slips from my hands.

I was not well connected. I hardly knew any bigshots then. It was then that I thought of Ranjan's father, M.L. Wadhawan. He was a senior functionary in the Ministry of Finance, looking after the Revenue Intelligence Affairs of India. The errant industrialists and tax evaders dreaded him like the plague.

I mustered up the courage and went to his residence at Pandara Road after office hours. I explained my good and not-so-good news to Aunty. She listened patiently and asked me to wait. The *intezaar* became like the wait of an *aashik* for his beloved, with a thousand thoughts crossing my mind.

Uncle reached home around ten pm.

'*Huzoor, yahan kaise. Kheraiat to hai?*' when I touched his feet. This was because Ranjan was in the States, and there was no reason to be there where I was at this late hour unless it was vital.

'*Munda pehli baar Japan ja reys hega hor ere kol passport nahi hega. Kuch karo eda. Pehli baar Hindustan de bahar ja reya hega,*' Aunty interjected on my behalf.

'*Kamaal da banda hega hain tu. Japani company vich kam karda yan hor tere kol passport nahi hega,*' he mocked. I was utterly dejected. '*Kado jaana ya?*'

'*Parson, Uncle,*' I responded chicken-heartedly.

'*Kee!* Impossible ya. *Roti khadi?*'

'*Haanji, Uncle.*'

'*Hun, tun ghar ja.*'

I had a bad night. I was sleeping when the phone rang.

'*Rishi, main Manmohan bol raya yan.*'

'*Kaun Manmohan?*' I asked in my sleep as I did not know any Manmohan.

'*Tere dost, Ranjan da father.*'

I was wide awake as *mantris* and bureaucrats are when they get a call from the PMO.

'*Tu dheek 10 baje apnian 2 photos hor age proof certificate le ke pahunch jain mere dafter. Late na hoin. Main bahut busy han.*' I jumped out of bed like a chimpanzee.

The following day, things moved at supersonic speed, and I had my passport in hand in about three hours. It was sheer magic or like the goal of Madonna, Hand of God. I visited Japan many times after that and twenty-four other countries. But the first visit was like your first love, which you never forget.

Wadhawan Uncle is no more, but he will always have a special place in my heart. Forever. He was a *farishta* for me.

Valentine's Day at Connecting Lives

Crores of rupees must have been spent today by the lovelorn. My wife and I, along with Prof. Avinash, had an out-of-the-world experience with the kids of Archna Tiwari, a 28-year-young child at her NGO.

Meandering through the narrow and dingy lanes of Azadpur reminded me of the lanes of the novel *Oliver Twist* and the film *Slumdog Millionaire*. Dogs, hens, and buffalos formed the reception committee, but once inside, we were transported to a vibrant, energetic, and beautiful world where education was being imparted to the deprived children of labourers living in small shanties sans bathrooms next to the nearby railway track. Archna, a former model-turned-special-educator, has made it her mission to help improve their lives.

While the kids of the elite schools of Delhi have all they need, the kids here aspire for new dresses, water bottles, and lunch boxes. The MHO provides free meals, fruit, and milk to these kids during their study hours.

We were amazed to learn that the kids remembered their first Metro ride and enjoying a hamburger. They are taught to wash their hands before and after meals and keep their surroundings clean. I was bowled over by the washroom, which was at par with a five-star hotel. The limited space has been utilised fully. The noble work being done by Archna speaks volumes of the tremendous effort that has gone behind running this venture.

A humbling experience indeed. I request readers who offer money at the house of God to open their purses for this educational mandir. I am sharing the bank details of the NGO for your reference. Believe me, friends, it will give you more happiness than a meal at Maurya, Taj, or a pleasure trip to Bali.

Bank Details:
Name of the Bank: State Bank of India
Account no: 38782796101
IFSC: SBIN0005997
Name: Connecting Lives
Branch: GTK Road, Azadpur

Wisdom from Krishna— The Sporty CEO Coach

Arjun had Krishna in *The Mahabharata*. I have my friend, Krishna, in this world to seek advice. He is a reticent young man of 60. He enunciates each word slowly, with clarity and deep meaning. He is a straight shooter when it comes to people he is close with. He has a knack for communicating lucidly and is extremely fit. He has an enviable IIT-IIM tag below his belt.

He has attained top positions in the corporate world and has become a CEO Coach now. He runs the Intrad School of Executive Coaching in Bangalore and the Kinesis Tennis Academy. As a certified tennis coach, he runs one of the best academies because tennis is his passion. He juxtaposes his vast knowledge from the corporate world with the sports arena for the young and the young at heart.

Here are some wise words he has shared with me over the years.

'Change cannot be forced on anyone. When it has to happen, it will happen. Whenever change happens, the person changing is in turmoil. It is a Hamlet-like situation. Rishi, you were pursuing your profession, i.e., international trading, and passion, i.e., sports, at the same time. I felt that you were playing cricket with a hockey stick. You were moving forward in the business world, but your head was always turned back to see the possibility of your full-time involvement in sports.'

'Your friends find you too decent. They feel you want to do well for everybody and tend to do things for free. Your wife feels that she married a Gandhi but did not want a Gandhi. The hard knocks of life must have taught you some invaluable lessons.'

'You should invest in yourself and your family.'

'You must have realised that your heart is bigger than your head. You need to shrink your heart and expand your head.'

"Your family, as a rule, has been right, and you, as a rule, have been wrong in judging people and situations.'

'You should start looking for opportunities from level 3 contacts that do not judge you.'

'You need to recharge your batteries. It is important for you to learn new things. You need to improve your knowledge, skill set, and behaviour.'

'Majority of your decisions have been emotional. They need to be rational.'

'You should always project a positive image of yourself.'

'You need to be humble. I have seen that most humble people are reticent folks. They don't have to prove themselves.'

'In order to act your way into a new way of thinking, you need to discover yourself—the real you.'

'You should resist temptations to change everything in one step. Instead, you should go for small wins.'

'You have to look for people who are what you want to be in the future.'

'You have been running after fame. You need to run after fortune also. It could be through writing or business. The ethical way.'

'Do something that keeps you happy. Writing certainly does. Pursue it with passion and full-time devotion. Have focus, and you will definitely succeed.'

Thank you, Krishna Kumar. I have only one word. Grateful.

Platform+Opportunity+Initiative = Impact

Getting applauded at the funeral of Sayeed Mohammad Mehndi. I consider myself blessed and fortunate to be a part of the memorial service of Mehndi Uncle on the 14th January, 2015, at Ghalib Auditorium in Delhi. I shared a more than fifty-year bond with the family as his son Feroz and I stayed near each other's houses in Karol Bagh and studied at Springdales School, Pusa Road.

When Praveen, a close common friend, shared the sad news, my eyes became moist. I called Feroz and told him I would take five minutes on the mike at the memorial service. 'Sure, why not, Rishi.' I started having pangs of nervousness when I saw the speakers who came before me. I was bowled over by their eulogies and realised a little later in life that, unknowingly, I had missed an opportunity of extracting pearls of wisdom from an icon. It was a typical case of *ghar ke saath Ganga beh rahi ho aur tum uske darshan na karo.*

Mark Tully used a phrase for him that he said was misquoted very often. 'Mehndi Saab was a real gentleman.' His wife Gillian, who spoke fluent Urdu, addressed him as Mamu Jaan and added an extremely emotional tone with her voice that he was *Laajawaab Mama and mujhse bahut pyar karte the.'* She shared with the august audience, which had renowned writers and academicians from Pakistan, that *'Mein Mamu Jaan ko bahut pyar karti thi. Voh Awadh ki tasveer ki ek achchi imarat thay.'*

S. Naqvi, whose mother was the sister of Mehndi Uncle, added in his speech, *'Kitne khush kismat hain hum ki hamein Mamu ke saath rehne ka aur waqt guzaarne ka saubhagya prapt hua.* Mamu Jaan was a writer, a playwright, a critical thinker, a social activist and a good-hearted person.' He said that an era had finished with the demise of Mehndi Mamu.

Azeez, a renowned artist from Pakistan, added, *'Woh log badnaseeb hain jinko Mehndi Saab ke saath rehna ka mauka nahin mila.'* Another Pakistani academician ended his poignant speech with *'Humein fakar hai ke humne Mehndi Saab ko dekha.'*

I was in a trance. I was glued to my seat, trying to absorb as much as I could about the extraordinary man who seemed extremely ordinary to me. I did not expect at all that I would be called on the stage. I had given up hope, and just as I was fighting a losing battle with my bladder after hearing the mesmerising speeches by ten stalwarts, the master of ceremonies announced my name. I tripped over a gent while making my way from my row and walked nervously to the stage. I did not utter a word for a few seconds which seemed like an eternity. I looked up and asked Waheguruji to give me strength. He did not let me down.

'Good evening, friends. I start with two major handicaps. I do not know Urdu and feel like a pygmy standing in front of galactico stalwarts who have spoken before me. But I have an advantage over several of you except the close immediate family members. I am among the blessed few who share a bond of more than fifty years with the Mehndi family. My house in Dev Nagar, Delhi, was very near the residence of Feroz. I met Mehndi Uncle for the first time when I was in the fourth standard and was a part of the birthday celebrations of Feroz. I would visit the Mehndi house often to study with Feroz as he was far more intelligent than me, and my parents thought that their *anpad ladka* would gain some knowledge from the Mehndi *parivar* that comprised intellectual giants. My father was aware of the fame of Mehndi Uncle and had seen his play *Ghalib Kaun Tha*. The elder sisters of Feroz, Zulfia and Shireen, had made a name for themselves at Springdales.'

'I was less interested in the study part and more in the excellent *biryani* and *kaleji,* which Zahira Aunty prepared with love and affection. Uncle would sit with us for a while, make small talk, listen more and talk less, but what set him apart was his serene demeanour and crisp white *kurtas.* He seemed to have imbibed the humility of the sages. We accompanied him to Sapru House a few times, but I could not absorb the enormity of his intellect then.'

'Though I saw *Ghalib Kaun Tha* when I was in my forties, I have come to know today that he was the original founder of the theatre group IPTA. I learnt, on that day, that our late President Zakir Hussain requested Uncle to write the play on Ghalib.'

'There are a few things in life which money cannot buy. They are goodwill, respect, honour, love, and integrity.

You have to earn them. You cannot buy them. Mehndi Uncle earned all accolades. I have only one regret. I expressed a keen desire to Feroz two years ago, when he came to India from Canada, that I wanted to visit Aligarh to meet Mehndi Uncle and Zahira Aunty. Call it my laxity, call it my ill luck. It was not to be.'

'The only silver lining is that when I am called by God and go to heaven, I will surely catch up with both, relish the tasty *biryani* and *kaleji* of Zahira Aunty and imbibe the pearls of wisdom which I missed on Earth from Mehndi Uncle. Thank you.'

There was a round of applause. I realised that my eyes had become moist. Quite a few of the audience came up to me to compliment me for my from-the-heart speech. They included Saed Naqvi, Political Editor of *Outlook*, Saba Naqvi, Azeeb Bhai, and others. I walked up to Mark Tully, who had walked up the stage with a stick with great grit and perseverance. I had read his works and seen him often on TV.

'Good evening, Sir. I desire to shake hands with you.' I held his hand warmly, with both my hands.

'You speak very well, Rishi. You spoke from the heart.' I was thrilled but kept my exuberance to myself. 'What do you do, Rishi?'

'I am an accidental author, and my second book is coming out shortly.' I gave a short, crisp presentation and ended with the request, 'I request you to be there at my launch.'

'Intimate me about ten days in advance, and I will surely make it if your launch date does not clash with my schedule.'

V. Murali—Dynamism and Charisma Personified

Murali means flute in Sanskrit. This is another name for the Hindu God Krishna, given to him because he played the flute.

Murali can carry on with others for joy, has a receptive nature, and bears the burden of others. Pragmatic, thorough, strong-willed, practical and stubborn at times, intuition and patience, and the ability to nurture others are other traits of Murali. All of them fit with a perfect T with V. Murali.

He came to Delhi by chance and was picked up by Marubeni Itochu, a Japanese Trading Company that saw his talent, drive and sincerity. God was on his side when Marubeni Itochu

Corporation decided to open a principal office in Chennai. Murali was the most suitable candidate. He adjusted as a fish adjusts to water. He knew the steel business, was very thorough in technical details, and had excellent negotiation skills.

He struck gold in the form of big business. Accolades followed him like bees follow honey, but he remained a simple man at heart and frugal in his habits. His good luck charm wife, Viji, acts as a jammer and brings him to the ground whenever he tries to fly. A made for each other couple on the lines of the Shah Rukh Khan film *Rab Ne Bana Di Jodi.*

Even though he stays at the Lalit or Hyatt Hotel when he comes to Delhi, which is quite often, we make it a point to have our *chaat* or *thali* at Nathu's Sweets at Bengali Market or the canteen across the Hyatt on Ring Road. We go down memory lane and delve into our times, the good and the not-so-good, and have a laugh afterwards.

Our conversation ends with, '*Bhai, yehi duniya hai.* If you are doing well, the world is good to you; if not, the world ignores you.'

Murali and I have had many ups and downs in life. We have weathered many a storm. God made us come out of the storm in a better, fitter, and livelier state. Both of us profess by the lines:

'Khistian sabhi kinare pe pahunch jati hai
Na jinta koi na ho uka khuda hota hai
Wahi hota hai jo manzoore kudha hota hai.'

Mona Singh—PhD in Spreading Happiness!

Mona Singh is less than half my age but has a maturity far beyond her years. She is beautiful in and out. She keeps her dresses classy, just like her thoughts, and is far from pretentious. Mona's amazing drive guides her life and makes her convert the impossible into possible. She has made *booras* revisit their *jawani* with her joy for life.

She cannot help but make hearts younger. She can give you an enticing tour of youth to people even at the age of 80. Even when she doesn't use words, she says a lot. I feel that God has sent her to earth to spread happiness. I can foresee her being invited by an Ivy League University to give a lecture on Happiness. She is still very young and has a long way to go.

Mona enjoys what she is doing, putting her heart and soul into it. She works like an ace director; unique and different because she can easily adjust and interact with people twice her age. She hugs everyone with genuine warmth and possesses commitment and passion in plenty.

She has worked tirelessly to build The Senior Saga, a group that makes excellent documentaries on senior achievers they can leave as a legacy. It is a vibrant body that gathers the no longer young folks who yearn for youth. It is a Mona Singh show all the way. She is assisted by a very able team, with Shreya looking after the IT and Satya handling photography. It is the CSR initiative of a visionary young man, Mr Gupta.

A few months ago, she prepared a *yaadgaar* ten-minute documentary on me and my art of writing. Like an adept sculptor, she also shot a thirty-second clip of my wife and me, which got 25,000 views. This is sheer happiness.

May 31st was a very special day as a melody was born that brought music into the lives of people who had forgotten youth and were taking slow, trepidant steps towards Nigambodh Ghat. I am one of them. Thank you, Mona *beta,* for the generosity of your *beeg dil* and kindness. You will always rock!

I have a hidden agenda in wishing Mona a Happy Birthday in advance. I am worried that her family, young friends, and *boora* well-wishers will not give me a chance. Happiness always, Mona!

Guneet—My Inspiration Engine in My Journey of the Battle of the Bulge

Venue—St. Sundari College. I was happy and depressed at the same time. Happy because it was the first time I entered the hallowed corridors of a girl's college, where the minimum percentage for entry was 99 percent. I was depressed when I saw the bright young scholars entering the college gates. They were smart and radiated a glow in their eyes.

I thought each girl looked at my rotund tummy, which was trying its best not to fall to the ground. They giggled and moved on to attend their classes. I was sure they had given me a sobriquet, Sardar Peepa Singh, and I felt awful.

The guard, who assumed he was Fort Knox's head gatekeeper, stopped me at the gate. 'Do you have an invite?'

'No, I don't.'

'Then you can't enter.'

'E tere pyo da college hai?' I thundered, seething angrily.

'Ab mein tere ko andar nahin jaane doonga.' I became the cynosure of all eyes.

A beautiful girl with dimples and long, jet black hair and hazel eyes wearing tight jeans and a white *kurti* and Clarks shoes stepped towards me.

'Sir, I am Guneet. I will take you in.' I was stunned but very elated. God had certainly been kind.

'I am Rishi, *beta*. Thank you very much, and God bless you.' She smiled. Very rarely had a young beauty smiled at me. Maybe girls did not like my dark Othello-type face and my *motappa*.

She took me straight to the front row VIP row and asked me to sit there.

'We have to meet again, *beta*. Can I invite you for lunch at the Triveni in front of FICCI in CP tomorrow at 12:30 pm, if you are free?'

'Sure, and I will give you a few tips on weight and waist reduction, Uncle, as I reduced from 98 kilos to 62 kilos in about two years'. I nearly jumped off my seat and hugged her. She was embarrassed but did not show it.

I was fifteen minutes late. Huffing and puffing as I was, she was waiting for me when I reached Triveni. She sprung up from her seat and touched my feet. I was truly touched.

'I have to nurture and strengthen this relationship,' I told myself. 'Let's order food first, and then we can talk.'

'I will order for you.' She did not ask about my occupation. I was so glad because I had none.

'Uncle, if you want to lose weight, you must make firm decisions. Say goodbye to sugar. If it is impossible, initially have one spoon in total per day.

'What!' I exclaimed. 'It is impossible, *beta*. I am a die-hard foodie who loves sweets.'

'Uncle, you will have to do it! *Jannat paane ke liye bahut kuch khona parta hai.*

- Say no to carbonated drinks.
- If you take canned juice, take it with 50 percent water.
- Avoid taking liquids by straw.
- Avoid carbohydrates. They convert into fat.
- Stop taking meals after eight pm.
- Start slow walking initially, increase it gradually and eventually start running.
- Hire a yoga teacher.

'My wife was a yoga teacher for thirty-six years in a government school, *beta.*' Now it was her chance to be shocked.

'What! Why didn't you take advantage of her? It's like *ghar mein Ganga beh rahi ho aur tum darshan na karo.* Start tomorrow at five am sharp and do it seven days a week without fail. I do not know why, Uncle, but I have taken a great liking for you and have a keen desire to make you a young, smart, handsome man again, even at the age of sixty-five. You certainly don't want to die young as you must have many responsibilities. I will monitor your progress regularly. I will meet you once a fortnight on a Saturday at Triveni to see if you are becoming smart.'

'Many thanks, *beta.* I will use only one word—grateful,' I responded as tears of joy came to my eyes.

'Hayaat mushtakil gum ke siva kuch bhi nahin,
Khushi bhi aati hai to aansoo ban kar aati hai.'

'Sorry, Uncle. I have a prior engagement and must leave, but we will touch base regularly.'

She touched my feet once again, and I was embarrassed. I felt like touching hers because she had become my guru.

Friends, I have started sharing my monthly progress report of my Battle with the Bulge since the 15th of February and shall continue to share it till I achieve my GOAL. The results in the 1st month have been phenomenal. I have lost 3.75 kgs and 1.5 inches around my waist. Hurrah!

If any of my readers has a similar goal, please share, as the biggest room in the world is the room for improvement, and I am desperate to reduce my shapeless shape.

Yoga for Torontowalas

It is fascinating to discover some good people by chance. I was enjoying my special *thali* with *bhhallas* at Haldiram Lajpat Nagar when I spotted a young, beautiful, fit girl with a *beeg* smile on her face enjoying something on her cell phone. I could not resist myself, left my lunch and lunged towards her.

'Sorry, *beta,* but it is rare to come across smiling faces in this sullen world.' She looked up and gave a bigger smile.

'I was enjoying watching memes.'

'Why don't you make them yourself?'

'But I don't know technology, Uncle?'

'So what. You can start learning right away. Why don't you sit with me, *beta?* What do you do in life?

'I am a yoga teacher in Toronto, and when I am in Delhi, I teach yoga at Ozone Defence Colony.'

'Wow! My wife is a yoga teacher too.' I beamed with pride.

'Then you shouldn't be so fat and should not eat what you are eating.' She looked at me with concern.

'I do that when I am outside the house. I have a weakness for food.'

'Then you should join my online classes. They are free.'

'Sure, *beta*. God bless you.'

Friends, please open *yogawithdisha.com*. You will be hooked. I was.

The yoga brain drain has started. India's loss is Canada's gain. Why? A yoga teacher earns $80 per hour in Canada. In India, I do not know. No wonder. Start right away, and you will gain a lot. Weight and waist reduction laced with *khushi* unlimited.

Twisha—Glittering!

She was silent like the calm sea. Her arms were wide open like champions after victory—a la Neeraj Chopra and Dhoni style. She was glittering like gold. She was beauty personified sans any make-up. Her brown eyes sparkled like diamonds. Her broad smile and confidence would give an inferiority complex to Priyanka Chopra and Deepika Padukone. My eyes could not resist watching her with unlimited love. I smiled at her. She smiled back. She was hardly six months young.

'Can I have the proud privilege of holding the future Olympic Gold medallist in my arms?' The mother, who was equally beautiful and vibrant, beamed with pride.

'Sure, Uncle. How did you know that I desire Twisha to focus and excel in sports rather than waste time just studying? Are you a *jyotish?*'

I kept mum as the proud mother handed the child into my arms. A lot of energy was instantly transferred to me.

The keenly observant child looked at me curiously as if I was someone from another planet. I assumed that she had not seen a Sardar in a turban. She maintained her swagger and kept on smiling. I experienced tons of happiness in a short while.

'What keeps you busy besides motherhood, *beta?*'

'I am a PhD scholar in Berlin and took a sabbatical when Twisha was born.'

'Wow! You are taking the champ to the land of champions. Your campus will surely have a playground, and Twisha can practice there. Just like Roger Federer started learning rudimentary tennis when he was not even four.'

'Why not?'

I blessed the child and the mother by putting my right hand on their heads. My day was made. May Twisha live up to her name and glitter and make her parents and India proud one day. God bless her.

My Love-Hate Relationship with Yoga!

I hated yoga for years, like Ukraine and Russia detest each other now. I assumed that only oldies engaged in this amusing pastime and also that I would never get old. The tragicomedy of my life was that, by a quirk of fate, I married a yoga teacher. She tried her best to get me interested in this cosmic energy-giving miracle, which would get me nearer to God, but failed miserably. I started loving my wife after a while, but my hatred for yoga continued.

When my health deteriorated, which was a gift from the corporate world forcing me to take about fifteen tablets a day, my *sarkar,* i.e., my wife, panicked and hired an exclusive yoga teacher for me. Acharya Shiv was an excellent guru, but I was a lousy *shishya.* He used to reach our house at six am sharp every day. However, I was never ready; about fifteen minutes were wasted daily. I used to perform my *aasanas* with a heavy heart. I squandered a lot of time asking Shiv about his air hostess and corporate big-wig clients. My wife used to get mad.

I was advised to reduce my food intake and shun sugar and sweets, but I couldn't. After tolerating me for six months, Shiv told my wife, *'Main Rishi ka kuch nahin kar sakta'* and he left for good.

My never-say-die-wala-attitude wife restarted teaching yoga to me. She had no choice. She did not want to become a widow soon. She gave the example of Dhirendra Bhramchari and Ramdev, who took yoga to the world and got the *goras* hooked on it. So much so that it is a US $16 billion industry in the US alone.

I had a brain wave. 'We should open a school in the US or start taking online classes.'

'There is no need. We are happy as we are,' she retorted. My dream project was nipped in the bud even before take-off.

As a rule, I am never jealous of people, but I am very jealous of my friend of thirty-five years, Honey Sharma. She is a strict yoga practitioner. Cleopatra-like, age has not withered her, and she looks twenty years younger than she is. She can easily perform the difficult *sheesh aasana* of standing upside down on her head. My protruding tummy barely lets me stand erect on my two feet. Discipline, dedication, and *mehnat ki baat hai.* They were never my strong points.

I am delighted that India is displaying its soft power to the world through yoga. UNO has officially declared 21st June as International Day of Yoga. The government needs to introduce yoga as a subject in all schools and colleges. Yoga was introduced in Delhi government schools only for one year, i.e., in 1983 when my wife became a yoga teacher. There were no recruitments after that. It needs to kickstart immediately; otherwise, the kids will become couch potatoes like I was and will be in the deep shit I am in presently, healthwise.

Meek Husbands!

Jesus said, 'Blessed are the meek.' He knew what he was talking about.

I am a very meek husband and am proud of this fact. *'Agar jhukne se ghar mein shaanti bani rehti hai to jhuk jaao.'*

This became the topic of our discussion at the diner, Lama's Place in Hauz Khas, where our humble heart surgeon friend Dr Rajesh Sharma invited us yesterday. My wife considers him as God on Earth.

'Kuch seekho, Rajesh Bhai *saab se.* He treats Honey as tenderly and lovingly as he treats the kids he operates on. He listens to her, helps her, sits with her every day despite his choco blocked schedule, and assists her in performing the *sheesh aasana* every morning. That is why she is still beautiful like Rekha and looks thirty years younger than her age. And you! You hardly do anything.'

Honey giggled. I looked at my dear and only wife and the ideal couple. Meekly. *Meri bhookh mit gayi.*

She was in her true element and added, 'Sudha Murthy, the philanthropist writer and wife of the billionaire industrialist Narayana Murthy at heart and pocket, said recently that her daughter made her husband pray every day and fast every Thursday. I could make my husband only a businessman, but my daughter could make hers the Prime Minister of the UK.'

I do not know Rishi Sunak personally. I will request my wife to l he is a meek hubby or not—only if she can fix an appointment. She controls my appointments, my purse strings, and my life.

'Girls are Better than Boys.' - Bhola Saab

It is my habit to interact with ordinary folks. They teach you important lessons about life which B schools don't. One day, I took an e-rickshaw to my residence, and the *vaahan chaalak* sparked my curiosity. He had a dishevelled look, his stubble was white, and he seemed about 70. I felt that he had a lot on his shoulders. He gave a weak smile. I smiled back.

'Aap paani piyen ge, bhai saab?'

'Haanji.'

'Aap ke bache aap ke saath rehte hain aur kya voh aap ki madad karte hain?'

He started talking. He said that he worked very hard to make his son a graduate, but after marriage, he separated and stayed close by but did not meet him at all. No phone calls either.

'Aadar nahin karta.' His eyes gleamed when he mentioned his daughters. They were married and kept in close touch with him, enquired about him, and met him when they could.

'Ladkiyan ladkon se zyada achi hoti hain,' and his eyes became moist. I hugged him warmly.

'Bhagwan sab dekh raha hai. Aap ke ache din aayen ge.' He touched my feet. I felt embarrassed.

'Sirf apni biwi ke paanv chuo, voh bhi jab tumhare mata pita saamne na hon.' He laughed loudly. As I always do, I gave him extra *bhaara* for a cup of tea with more milk. My day started on a good note. Bhola was only 50 years old.

Paradise of Love

More than 2000 enthusiastic fans were enjoying the dance performance by the Naga girls on the stage of the open auditorium at the Pragati Maidan during the World Book Fair. The couple sitting next to me were in their own Garden of Eden. Just as athletes are in their zone, so were they.

'*Beta,* are you in love with her?' My sudden question stunned the boy. He was stumped, stupefied, flabbergasted, and did not know what to say.

'And you, *beta.* Do you love him?'

'Yes, Uncle, I do.' The reply was prompt. I liked her confidence.

'Do you want to marry him?'

'Yes, I do.'

'Has he written any love letter to you?'

'No, he hasn't,' she responded with slight pain in her eyes.

'Why, young man? How many years have you been together?'

'More than two years.' It was the first time he opened his mouth.

'Ram is fond of writing.' It was the first time I got to know his name.

'Okay, I will assist him. I am good in this field.'

'Ohh. Did you, too, have a love marriage?'

'No, *beta,* I was a failure in love,' I responded with morose, pitiful eyes. 'I was not so lucky, but I am happy,' I responded while introducing myself and exchanging cell numbers.

I got up, hugged the kids warmly and sauntered towards the metro station. I was happy that I had done one good deed today. I smiled while walking and blessed the kids in my heart.

Ignorance, Ignorance, Ignorance!

I have still not mastered the art of speaking the right thing at the right place and time. I do not know what, how, and when to speak, and I have made a fool of myself many times.

We went to the wedding of the daughter of a very close friend, Murali, to Chennai. It was a grand affair. More than 1500 guests had congregated for the happy occasion. I loved the wedding because Murali and his wife, Vijji, accorded the same respect to ordinary guests like us as to the Japanese and VIP CEOs who had flown down from Japan, the USA, Singapore, Delhi and Mumbai.

A typical South Indian dinner on leaves was served to the guests seated in a long line of seating like in a college mess. I found it unique. Typical of Murali, who has always kept a low profile and commanded much respect and love from friends worldwide.

We happened to get a seat right next to a gorgeous girl and a handsome young boy.

'Are you Siddharth, who played the role of Bhagat Singh in *Rang de Basanti?*'

'Yes,' he responded with utmost modesty and a broad smile.

'Your acting was terrific, and you suited the role perfectly. Can my wife and I get a photo with you after dinner?'

'Sure.' I was happy because it was my first photo with an actor.

Just as the photo was about to be clicked, I asked the girl to join us too.

'*Beta,* you are very beautiful and should enter films.' The girl, with quiet confidence, smiled and joined us sportingly.

It was only when we returned to Delhi, and I flaunted my photo with Sidharth to my daughter, that I came to know that the girl I had advised to join films was none other than the talented actress and heartthrob of young men at St. Stephen's Delhi and India, Aditi Rao Hydari.

Money, Money, Money!

Fans worldwide went wild over the famous Abba song many years ago. Millions are crazy even now to make tons of money. Money talks loudly in this what's-in-it-for-me *matlabi duniya.* Everything else walks at a slow, lethargic pace of an old person. That is the tragedy of life. Folks will do anything for more money—cheat, drop friends, relatives and whatnot.

I have a close friend who studied in Japan when he was young, as his father was posted there. He went to a good college in Delhi and got a decent job. His life became hell when he married, as his world and his wife's world were antithetical. He lost a lot of money in the divorce case and his job and went into a deep depression. He became dependent on his brothers after his parents passed away. He had cancer and was not insured. He lost a lot of money in the treatment.

The greedy real brothers were confident that he would not survive. They had their eyes on an expensive flat he owned in South Delhi. When he was very ill, they managed to get his signature for property transfer in their name after his demise.

'My brothers are only interested in my money and want me to die soon. I have lost the will to live. I am bored with life.'

The worst bankrupt in the world is a person who has lost enthusiasm. My friend has lost his enthusiasm. I cheer him up by telling him that his brothers could go before him and they can take all the money with them to hell. He smiles.

Coco Chanel, which costs a lot of money, may give the scent, but does it add to the aura or personality? I met three Indian billionaires during my professional innings, but they did not impress me as much as a billionaire sans money who created a powerful impact with his work and humility. Dr Abdul Kalam, the ex-President of India, used only one room out of the 300-plus rooms in Rashtrapati Bhavan when he resided there.

Making money should not become the sole motive of your life. When you die, people will not remember you for your money but for the good that you have done. How many hearts have you touched? Money is a funny thing. It can get you all the comforts, but it cannot get you good health or good genuine friends. Focus on this critical aspect more. Be content with what you have. Don't run after money; otherwise, it will make you run out of precious life before your time. You can certainly enjoy life sans too much money too. Just do it.

Smile—It Costs Nothing!

Smile Instructors are raking in big money in Japan. The crescent-eyed, round-cheeked Japanese get training in the Art of Hollywood smiles. Regular classes are being held, and the smile teachers are smiling all the way to the bank. I am surprised. Why do you have to pay to concoct a smile? You can see the face of a smiling child and get all the thrills.

You may not have a reason to smile, but your smile can undoubtedly bring a smile to someone's face. Once, we were entering the VFS counter, which issued visas, and my authoritative wife was giving me instructions.

'*Tenu gappan maaran di aadat hai.* Don't start your small frivolous talk there, or we will be denied our visa. Answer only relevant questions.' I forgot her orders.

I smiled. The smart, confident, no-nonsense girl across the counter smiled back. 'Why are you going to the UK?'

'I am following my wife. I will go wherever she goes, and I will be going there after thirty-three years if the embassy gives me a visa.'

The girl couldn't help but smile again. I got talking. I asked her name and how she found her job. She was a sport. 'May you live up to your name, Neha *beta,* and spread love around,' I said as I departed. I was so engrossed in my talk that I left all the important documents behind. Neha had to request someone to rush after me. I still haven't got my visa.

I smile at walkers who cross me during my leisurely stroll in the morning, at e-rickshawalas, auto and cab drivers, and even at the people sitting in the vehicle across mine at the red light. Invariably they return the smile. I feel that I have done a good deed. This morning, I smiled at a lady sorting vegetables at the store. She smiled back.

'Happy morning and an awesome day.'

'You too.' I was pleased but realised I had forgotten my walking stick at the store when I reached home. I smiled and walked back to retrieve it.

My school friend Ron Wadhawan based in Texas, has a dog, Ginger, whom he treats as a daughter. Ginger makes his life more wonderful, accompanying him in choosing wines, shopping, and broadening his smile daily. She makes his life worth living. Is it her smile which turns him on? I will ask her if she comes to India.

Politeness Pays—Tanya of Indigo Airlines

It is fascinating to discover some people in life. I boarded the 50-minute flight from Kolkata to Aizawl, Mizoram, at one pm. The two air hostesses started the safety drill for the benefit of the passengers, who seemed oblivious to the same.

The beautiful girl standing next to me could have easily been an actress. I volunteered to assist as she could not find a suitable place to keep her equipment.

'Can I hold it for you, *beta?*' She looked at me a little surprised, smiled and relented.

I had lunch at Kolkata airport and did not buy any food on the flight.

Once the service was finished, she came to me and said, 'Sir, do you need any tea, coffee, or sandwich? I will not charge you anything for the same.' I was stunned.

'Many thanks, *beta,* for your kindness, but I do not need anything.' She smiled and went to where her colleagues were standing.

After a while, she returned with two soft drinks and a sweet. 'These are for you, Aunty, and your daughter.' I was caught off-guard.

'But why, *beta?* You are being very kind. God bless you.' I touched her head to bless her.

'It is rare to come across people like you in this world. You addressed me as *beta,* and I was truly touched.'

'May life be full of more blessings, success, and happiness for you, Tanya *beta,*' I said after seeing her name tag on her sweater. My eyes became moist, and my day was made.

Goody-good Neighbours
Make Zindagi Haseen

The person who forgets the past forfeits the future. My mind went back 50 years when I received a jaw-dropping *dil khush karne wala* comment to my write up *Meek Husbands* from Sudeep Bhalla, whose family was our landlord in Dev Nagar West Delhi, where we resided.

'I really enjoy your articles, especially your vocabulary, even when not required, just like our honourable ex-Minister (he was referring to Shashi Tharoor). Knowing you since childhood, I always knew your potential. Like your dad (Pritam Singh, Founder Director Physical Education and Sports, Delhi University), you will be a great achiever.'

I was thrilled. Sudeep was my senior from Springdales School Delhi and lead guitarist of Rocking Springdales (the school band), along with Susmit Bose, the crooner who got worldwide acclaim as a singer. I vividly remember flying kites from our terrace. I will never forget his mother, Janaki Aunty's kindness when she took me to the hospital when I got burnt in a freak kitchen accident while my parents were at work. We did not have a TV then, and I used to watch the *Chitrahaar* melody of songs every Wednesday and a movie on Sunday in their drawing room, sitting on the carpeted floor with the AC on full blast when very few houses had this luxury.

I stay in a small colony called Ajay Enclave of less than 150 houses in West Delhi. It is the best colony in the world because I have wonderful neighbours who come to your help immediately in your hour of need.

When my mother passed away, our immediate neighbours were by our side at midnight. As I have stopped driving, Gurdeep and Babli, who stay right across our house, stopped everything and helped us fulfil all the last rites formalities. It was *deja vu* with Bobby when my father passed away.

A young, vivacious, well-read girl, Seema, who stays only two houses away, is Cheerleader No. 1 in my colony for my articles. She has given me a magic mantra for writing and tells me to focus on things I am good at and enjoy doing.

I make it a point to chat with young kids from 5-15 years while they wait for their school buses or play in the park. They make my *zindagi* more *haseen,* worth living and worth celebrating.

Stay closely connected with your neighbours. They will come faster for your help than relatives who stay far away.

Happy Birthday to the Teacher Who Encouraged Me to Write

Dr Reverend Valsan Thampu interviewed me for the English (Hons) course at St Stephen's 49 years ago.

'Do you think you will be able to cope with English?' One of the teachers asked me.

'Ye…yes Si, Sir. I wi…will be able to co-cope up with it,' I stammered.

'It is not cope up. It is cope with.' He looked at me with pity in his eyes.

'Are you fond of reading and writing?' A saintly teacher with kindness writ over his face asked me. My face gleamed.

'Yes, Sir. I am fond of both. A few articles of mine have been published in my school magazine.'

'Very good. Are you fond of reading?'

'Yes, I am, Sir. So much so that I have been caught reading interesting books during my classes.' Everyone laughed. So did I.

'What sort of books do you read?' the same teacher asked.

'I am fond of Khushwant Singh as I find him funny and bold. The way he builds his characters is very interesting. I want, sorry, desire to be like him one day. I also like inspirational stories.'

He smiled. 'Do you play any sport?'

'I am a sports enthusiast cum cheerleader at present, but I will take up a sport here if I am selected,' I replied confidently.

The wonder of wonders, I was selected. I took up athletics in college and excelled in it. I kept in touch with Thampu Sir. He used to jog in the morning with the students and play tennis after his classes. I am truly inspired by his sincerity, knowledge, commitment, drive, and love for students. He went on to become the principal of the college in 2007. I wrote a newspaper article on him, which was well appreciated and gave me tremendous happiness.

My father, Sardar Pritam Singh, was a great fan of his and went out of his way to help him end the strike by teachers and *karmcharis* dying for his ouster. They failed.

I am still in touch with him. He was kind enough to write the forewords for two of my books, *Roots Shoots Boots* and *Joy of Working with the Japanese.* He and his wife, Dr Grace, hosted my wife and me for a week when we visited Trivandrum in 2019. We loved it. I got the opportunity to sit at my guru's feet, discuss books and life with him, and gain more knowledge. He would get up at three am, read and write and become a farmer for two hours daily on his small land. It was Heaven on Earth.

People, as a rule, change their gurus and their girlfriends fast. I won't. I will keep Dr Thampu and my girlfriend, oops, my wife, like priceless treasures in the Fort Knox of my heart.

To more and more happy and youthful years ahead, Thampu Sir.

Is Old Age a Curse?

It was pouring. I was utterly drenched but enjoying the rain as I left the nearly empty park. My eyes did not miss the old Sardar sitting on the pavement with a plastic sheet covering the newspapers and magazines he was selling. He did not have an umbrella. I greeted him as I had done for many years.

'You should go home, *bhai saab.*'

'I can't afford to. *Roti naheen khaani.*'

'But don't your kids look after you?'

'No,' he responded with a pained look in his eyes. 'They sweetly talked me into transferring my property and assets in their name and have disowned me now.'

He was sixty but looked more than eighty, haggard and battered. This is the rotten life of many emotional oldies in India who act in haste and repent at leisure. They are living a slow, painful death which is not coming quickly.

Akelapan, i.e., loneliness kills you softly in old age. The selfish kids are busy leading their lovely lives—socialising, running up the corporate ladder, building houses, buying cars, and enjoying themselves. The irony is that they dote on their kids and ignore their parents. Strange indeed. I have come across many people rushing to India when their parents pass away, performing the last rites with fake faces, settling property issues in a tearing hurry, and zooming back to base. *Yahi zindagi hai.*

I am glad to have befriended a few who have loved and respected their parents. My business mentor, Mahadevan Anand, was brought to the ground many times by his mother, even when he became the chairman of his company. My school friend, Rajiv Sethi, learnt the ropes of business from his father and stayed in a house of four generations. He listened to his father till his last days and is replicating his best practices. It was *deja vu* with Dr Pramod Kohli, Praveen Kapoor, Gurmeet Grover and Surinder Verma. Ron Wadhawan left his work for 18 months in the USA when his parents were on their last legs in life's journey.

The presence of the elders is enough to build a blissful house. As you go up the steps of life, whether it is family or work, the role becomes less and less, but the importance of that role becomes more and more. You can rock and soar to the sky like an eagle when old age catches up with you if you are physically and mentally fit, have made the right investments at the right time, have friends, travel and cultivate the habit of reading, which shall make you new friends, live many lives and take you to lands you have never been to.

S.H. Raza was a world-famous modernist artist whose paintings commanded a price of $2 million in auctions. He went to Paris to study art in 1950, but he died alone in his small flat in Delhi with no one to look after him. His friends and relatives ran away with his paintings there and left him to rot, and it was the stink that made the neighbours call the police. What an ending to a royal life if this is true.

My father lived till the ripe age of 97. He was mentally alert. He did not deny age but defied it. He kept in touch with the youth and read voraciously. He sang songs of Heer Ranjha, Sassi Pannu, and Laila Majnu while having his Patiala peg of rum every evening. He enjoyed life to the hilt. He would always say,

'Sah ja maute kaalie mein aje na vela,
Hale mere jaan da nahion hoya vela.'

(Death, you have to still wait as I am very busy,
Time has not yet come for me to depart.)

The family celebrated his 100th birth anniversary on April 1, 2023, when the world-famous Chaar Yaar quartet paid a glowing tribute to him through their melodies. Thank you, Madan Gopal Singh *bhai saab,* lovingly called Mantoo, for making it possible. Papa would have surely enjoyed your singing in heaven.

I end with the immortal lines of one of the greatest philosophers of yester centuries Lucius Annaeus Seneca, 'As is a tale, so is life: not how long it is, but how good it is, is what matters.'

My dear oldies, make the most of your life because you never know *kal ho na ho.*

'Lai hayat aaye kaza le chali chale,
Na apni khushi se aaye na apni khushi se chale.'

PART XII

Battle of the Bulge

Last evening, I met my close friend, Dr Rajesh Sharma, a heart surgeon. Looking at my girth, he couldn't help asking me, 'What is your weight, and how much is your waist?'

'I haven't checked for the last three months, but it was 83 kgs then, and my waist was 43".'

'Let us check now,' he said with a concerned look. I nearly had a heart attack when I found that my weight had increased to 91 kg and my waist had become 46".

'Rishi, you are heading for big trouble. Reduce your weight by 10 kgs and your waist by 4 inches as soon as possible. You stand the risk of a heart attack, diabetes, sugar and very high BP.'

My heart started beating faster; the speed of my breath matched the speed of the Shinkansen Express in Japan.

'Change your lifestyle and start exercising.'

My father passed away at the ripe age of 97 and joked that he was worried because he feared that I would die before him and he would have to look after my kids. My mother used to say that even when I was dying, I would tell her, 'Mummy, please make my food first.' They were fit till the very end. I am only 65 years young at heart and desire to attain the century mark.

I called up my school chums Praveen Kapoor and Ranjan Wadhawan, who had reduced from 132 kg to 93 kg and 101 kg to 70 kg, respectively, by sheer grit and willpower. They gave me their pearls of wisdom and assured me that I could certainly succeed. Their words and Dr Rajesh Sharma's invaluable advice were music to my ears.

I request my readers, especially the ones who have become winners, to share their experiences as they will become inspiration engines for me.

Ms Chuk—My Nemesis

Chuk is the Punjabi word for severe back spasms, which hurt a lot.

Just as controversy looks me up often, loves and chases me, so does Ms Chuk. I have been avoiding her for two decades. However, she is relentless. She is infatuated with me and loves me immensely. She comes into my life unannounced sans any warning. She arrives when I am changing into my trousers or shorts or tying a turban.

Just as your *mashook* gives you sleepless nights, so does Ms Chuk. I can't sit properly, can't sleep properly, and can't wear my socks and shoes at all. My wife has to do these chores with a heavy heart and a frown, but she does it anyway.

Ms Chuk has made me lose the Battle of the Bulge. Completely. Outrightly. I am outfoxed, outmanoeuvred. I am frustrated.

'Ms Chuk aur mera rishta bhi bada ajeeb hai,
Tamaam umr saath rahe aur phir bhi twaraf na hua.' It is a tragic *rishta*.

My young, beautiful, sweet, efficient, and overworked physiotherapist, Avneet, calls me 'Peepa Uncle' because my 46-inch plus tummy is dying to fall to the ground.

'I desire to throw Ms Chuk out of my life as soon as possible. Please help me, *beta.*'

'You have back muscle spasms, Uncle. They are due to too much sitting, bad walking posture, and no exercise at all, especially stretching exercises. You should do yoga regularly. *Aap ke to ghar me* Ganga *beh rahi hai aur aap kuch faida nahin utha rahe.* Aunty is a yoga teacher. Take her help.'

I look at her sullenly. My wife glares at me.

'And you are old now. Age is catching up with you fast. It affects the body, and recovery takes time.'

'I'm not old yet,' I blurt out with a hurt face. The wise and intelligent physio smiles but keeps her mouth shut.

Friends, is Ms Chuk troubling you, and how are you keeping her away? Please help me.

Appreciation!

Kids, girls and boys, oldies, stars, and superstars want it. All yearn for it. I am dying for it. I want my readers to appreciate my writing. It motivates me. My positive hormones are energised. I become more vibrant and happy.

The GOAT (Greatest Of All Times), Novak Djokovic, has won his 23rd Grand Slam in tennis—10 Australian, 7 Wimbledon, 3 US Open, and 3 French on clay court, which is not his forte. Despite his funny court antics, the Joker, as he is called, has proved he is the best. He's outsmarted all his rivals. I am sure he didn't like it when the crowd at Roland-Garros acknowledged his victory grudgingly. They were upset that their hot favourite, Raphael Nadal, did not participate. This was lousy sportsmanship. They should have appreciated Novak's tremendous feat. They failed in this task.

Why?

From 1997-2010, I visited various swimming pools in Delhi, Chennai, Surat, Jaipur, and Mumbai, where my kids used to participate in inter-school or inter-state meets. I noticed a unique, peculiar pattern. The vociferous supporters, including teammates, teachers, coaches, and parents, would make a din for their near and dear ones but maintained a *maun vrat* for other participants during the race and at the prize distribution ceremonies. I was surprised.

I used to seize the initiative and request the organisers to let me be at the mike and assist the official announcer. Rarely did anyone say no. I played my part well. Using quotes from Shakespeare, *shayari,* and giving examples of stalwarts, I made it an inspiring, fun exercise. I exhorted the audience to clap for the winners as *'Sab bache saanje hote hain'* and reminded them that clapping cost nothing. I succeeded and was elated, which gave me loads of happiness. I made quite a few friends too.

I make it a point to appreciate cab drivers, *e-rickshaw chaalaks,* helpers, guards at colony gates, and waiters. I don't lose anything, but it makes my day brighter. Psychologists need to do a serious study on what makes people stop appreciating their not-so-young spouses. Change your mindset. *Dil barra kijiji,* and I assure you, you will be a gainer.

Good luck!

Wailing Kids and Pareshan Mothers!

It is common for me to see exasperated, stressed mothers trying to persuade their kids to alight their school buses in the morning.

A child, around five years young, was howling that he did not want to go to school. The mother, who was in her night suit and seemed in a rush, desperately tried to push him inside the bus. The conductor was pulling him hard, like in a tug of war, as he was getting late. I requested the mother, who did not know me, to let the kid take a holiday and chill at home.

'*Beta,* your child is not going for the board exam. Go to the school, meet his class teacher and find out why he is reluctant.' She looked at me and agreed.

Parents, primarily when both partners work and live as a nuclear family, face this peculiar challenge. They depend on helpers at home who pick up the kids from the bus stands in the afternoon. Their mind stays at home even while they are in the office. The rat race for your kid to be better than your neighbour's kids makes it seem like an Olympics competition. The heavy school bags, tuitions, and extra activities classes put a lot of load on the poor kids.

Is it all worth it? Absolutely not. The specs will come up fast, and sans any physical activity, the child may become a nerd but will not have a well-rounded, confident personality when grown up. Watching too many cartoons is another hindrance to proper and healthy growth.

Minimal interaction with parents is a fast track to becoming an introvert. When kids get all they demand by crying, they will not learn the value of money. They will have a really tough time facing the hard knocks of life.

I asked another group of mothers with kids in the 11-14 age group. 'Our kids want to run away from home. They feel they have too many restrictions there. They have friends in school and find their company better than ours.'

This is the tragicomedy of the life of the loving parents. Like birds leaving their nests, the children will leave their homes and parents to pursue their higher education and professions. The poor parents will be left to fend for themselves.

Do not put pressure on your kids. Otherwise, the following lines will hold true for you,

'Na khuda hi mila na visale sanam,
Na idhar ke rahe na udhar ke rahe.'

Printed by Libri Plureos GmbH in Hamburg,
Germany